A-Z ANIMALS
FOR THE CURIOUS ADULT

By Julie Eastman

Chapel Hill, North Carolina

Copyright © 2024 by **Julie Eastman**

All rights reserved. No part of this publication may be reproduced, distributed, or transmitted in any form or by any means without the author's prior written permission.

ISBN: 979-8-35094-285-9

INTRODUCTION

In 2020 I began a series of alphabet animal paintings using a combination of acrylic paints, rollers, stencils and brushes. Cutting stencils is a fascinating and enjoyable process, and a different stencil needs to be cut for each layer of color. Each animal took time to develop, and I often added brushwork for finishing touches. Once an animal was finished, I would share with friends and include a brief description about the animal. Originally my goal had not gone beyond completing the 26 animals and holding an exhibit in my community. But over the time of this project, I received many enthusiastic responses about both the paintings and how my friends enjoyed learning from the descriptions as well as much encouragement to do a book. I decided why not, and perhaps it was time for adults to have their very own A-Z animal book!

I hope you will enjoy the book as much as I have enjoyed putting it together. Finally, I am grateful to my husband Mike Sollins for all his support during this project, and I dedicate this book to him.

ABOUT THE AUTHOR

Julie Eastman paints in watercolor and acrylics. She has taught art courses for many years in local art centers and has held solo exhibits around Raleigh and Chapel Hill. As a member of the Orange County Artists Guild for ten years, she took part in the Guild's studio tour each year, opening up her studio and displaying current work to the community. Julie is now retired from teaching but continues to paint. She lives with her husband Mike Sollins in Chapel Hill, North Carolina.

NOTE TO THE READER

On the animal title headings I have listed alternate names when applicable and the scientific name. In the descriptions I have included the IUCN red list rating for each animal. IUCN stands for the International Union for Conservation of Nature, and the red list gives the global extinction risk status for animal, fungus and plant species. There are nine categories:

1. Not Evaluated
2. Data Deficient
3. Least Concern
4. New Threatened
5. Vulnerable
6. Endangered
7. Critically Endangered
8. Extinct in Wild
9. Extinct

The IUCN red list is used by government agencies, wildlife agencies, natural resource planners, and other groups interested in conserving biodiversity.

TABLE OF CONTENTS

Introduction iii
About the Author v
Note to the Reader vii
Alpaca *Vicugna pacos* 2
Bear *Ursus arctos* 6
Cow *Bos taurus* 10
Duck *Anas platyrhynchos* 14
Elephant *Loxodonta africana and Loxodonta cyclotis* 18
Fox *Vulpes lagopus* 22
Groundhog *Marmota monax* 26
Hippopotamus *Hippopotamus amphibius* 30
Ibis *Eudocimus albus* 34
Javelina *Dicotyles tajacu* 38
Koala *Phascolarctos cinereus* 42
Lynx *Lynx canadensis* 46

Mule *Equus mulus* 50
Nuthatch *Sitta canadensis* 54
Opossum *Didelphis virginiana* 58
Pika *Ochotona princeps* 62
Quail *Callipepla gambelii* 66
Rabbit *Sylvilagus floridanus* 70
Spoonbill *Platalea ajaja* 74
Turtle *Terrapene carolina* 78
Unau Sloth *Choloepus didactylus* 82
Vulture *Coragyps atratus* 86
Wolverine *Gulo gulo* 90
Xerus Squirrel *Xerus rutilus* 94
Yellow Tang *Zebrasoma flavescens* 98
Zebra Finch *Taeniopygia castanotis* 102
Sources 107

A-Z ANIMALS
FOR THE CURIOUS ADULT

ALPACA

Alpaca   *Vicugna pacos*

There are two breeds of alpacas. The Huacaya alpacas discussed here have a crimpy, sheep-like fiber and comprise about 95% of the species, and the remaining Suri alpacas produce a straight fiber that curls downward and looks like dreadlocks. Alpacas are herd animals from Peru that go far back in history. They are native to the Andes mountains in South America and are thought to have descended from the vicunas (the smallest of the camelid family). They were domesticated by the indigenous Andean people over 6,000 years ago. Alpacas were primarily treasured for their beautiful soft fleece, which was reserved to make fabrics for royalty. They were also bred for meat. The alpaca industry in Peru thrived for thousands of years and into the years of the Incan Empire before Spanish Conquistadors conquered the Incans in the mid-16th century. Surviving Incans fled to the inhospitable high Andes and took alpacas with them. The many alpacas left behind fared poorly. The Spanish preferred reserving their grazing land for sheep and cattle and slaughtered alpacas for meat. This practice, along with the diseases imported by the Spanish, almost annihilated the species.

In the 19th century, there was interest in Europe and Australia to find uses for the fine quality alpaca fibers, but commercial importation of alpacas did not begin significantly until the 20th century. In the 1960s, the Peruvian government launched a breeding program to improve the production of alpacas and the quality of their fleece. In the 1980s and 1990s, the United States, Canada, Australia, New Zealand, and England began to import alpacas. Today, alpacas have been exported all over the world, although the majority (about 3 million) remain in Peru and other countries in South America. All alpacas are domesticated; there are no wild alpacas.

The alpaca is slender with long legs, a long neck and pointed ears. It has excellent eye sight and hearing. Smaller than its relative, the llama, it has a height of about 3 ft. from the shoulder and weighs 100-200 lbs. The beautiful, soft, warm and hypoallergenic fleece that alpacas produce is their most notable trait, and it comes in 22 natural colors. Usually shorn once a year in the spring, the male produces about 8 lbs. of fiber and the female about 5 lbs. Males and females are similar in appearance, but males have larger incisors and canines (their fighting teeth). They do not have front/top teeth, so they can appear to have an underbite.

Alpacas are herbivores and eat pasture grass and hay, and they use communal dung piles, which help control parasites. Being herd animals, alpacas are social and live in family groups with a territorial alpha male, females and their young. Members follow a certain hierarchy, setting their own personal space and recognizing the dominant males in the different groups in the herd. They communicate with body language and a variety of sounds like humming, maternal clucking, snorts and alarm calls. They can also spit at each other when threatened.

Females can breed at 12-15 months and males at 30-36 months. Alpacas can breed any time of the year because the female experiences induced ovulation after mating. Males can mate with multiple females. The female usually gives birth to one baby, called a cria. Gestation is about 11.5 months. Newborn crias weigh 17-33 lbs. and can stand shortly after birth. They are weaned at 6-8 months. Because of their gentle and docile nature, alpacas can make good pets, but as herd animals, they need the companionship of other alpacas. The alpaca's lifespan is 15-20 years.

BEAR

Bear (Brown Bear, Grizzly Bear) *Ursus arctos*

The brown bear is widespread and has a world population of about 200,000, with many subspecies. While its range used to be larger, it is now found only in northern parts of North America and Eurasia. In North America, Alaska has about 32,000 brown bears, western Canada about 25,000, and the northwest United States about 650. Brown bears prefer open areas and have a varied habitat that includes coastal regions, river basins, alpine meadows, forests and the Arctic tundra. The brown bears discussed here are the coastal brown bears that live on the southern Alaskan and Canadian coast and the inland brown bears, also called grizzlies (because their outer hair is pale at the tips), that live in the interior of Canada, Alaska and parts of the northwest United States. Coastal bears are larger because of their access to salmon, and inland bears or grizzlies are smaller and are more vegetarian.

Brown bears vary in size and can be very large, with a body length of 5-9 ft. Males weigh 300-1,200 lbs. and females 175-550 lbs. They are usually dark brown with short rounded ears, small eyes, a long concave nose, a distinctive shoulder hump and big paws with long curved claws well adapted for digging. The claws, however, make it difficult for adults to climb, but their cubs can. Their hearing and sense of smell are excellent, but their eyes are weak. Brown bears walk on the whole soles of their feet at a slow, lumbering pace but can run fast in spurts and are excellent swimmers. They have vast overlapping home ranges in the hundreds of square miles, with range size related to food availability. They are not territorial but are very protective of their personal space.

Brown bears eat mostly a vegetarian diet of plants and berries but also fish, animals and carrion. While solitary, they may gather in groups where food is plentiful, such as salmon spawning rivers or garbage dumps. In groups, they follow a loose social hierarchy based on age and size to avoid serious conflict. Brown bears are mostly diurnal, active in the early morning and evening and at rest during the day. They can exhibit playful behavior, such as chasing birds and sliding down snow banks.

Many brown bears go into partial hibernation or torpor for 4-8 months if the winter is harsh and food is scarce. To prepare for this, they go into a state of hyperphagia in late summer when they continuously gorge themselves, acquiring a substantial layer of protective and nourishing fat. They dig dens, sometimes in a hillside or under tree roots, or they use other cavities like rock caves or hollow logs. In hibernation, their metabolism slows down, and they do not eat, drink, urinate or defecate. They can lose 30% or more of their body weight during hibernation.

The female reaches sexual maturity at 3 1/2 years and the male at 5 1/2 years, and the breeding season is early May to mid-July. Both sexes are promiscuous but serially monogamous and stay in pairs for a short time. The female's urine markings during estrus attract males. After mating, the blastocyst does not get implanted until about six months later, when the female begins hibernation. Gestation is 180-266 days from the time of mating. If the female has not accumulated enough fat reserves, implantation won't occur. If implanted, the mother gives birth in eight weeks in her den to tiny blind fur-less cubs (usually twins) that weigh about a pound. She nurses them until spring when they reach 15-20 lbs. and are ready to go out, forage, and learn survival skills from her. The cubs start eating a variety of food at five months, but the mother may continue to nurse them for another couple of years. The mother and cubs remain together for about three years and form strong bonds. Once the cubs leave, she is ready to mate again. Males play no parental role, and since they can actually be a threat, the mother is fiercely protective and avoids taking her cubs near them. Despite the mother's care, over 50% of cubs will not reach sexual maturity due to starvation, accidents and conflicts with other bears.

Brown bears are seed dispersers, which is good for the ecosystem. They tend to avoid humans but can be aggressive if surprised or with their young. They are hunted in Alaska and Canada's Yukon Territory but with strict regulations. While habitat loss continues, the brown bear's IUCN rating is of least concern, and their lifespan is 25-30 years in the wild, with some living longer.

COW

Cow (Charolais Cattle) *Bos taurus*

The exact origins of the Charolais breed are unknown. But it is speculated that their ancestors might have come from ancient Rome, partly because records mention religious sacrifices of white cattle and that the Romans brought them along when they invaded France. Later, there was literary reference to white cattle in the Charolais region around the town of Charolles as early as 868. Beginning in the 14th century, the Charolais region was fought over, and tariff barriers and customs duties were imposed until it was finally reunited with France in 1772. The resulting isolation of Charolais during this tumultuous period turned out to be beneficial to the Charolais cattle because the breed was strengthened and kept pure.

Little more is known until historical records show that the Charolais breed became popular in nearby towns like Lyons and Villefranche in the 16th and 17th centuries. In 1773, Claude Matthieu moved his Charolais herd to the region of Nievres, where truly significant breeding began. In 1864, a herd book was set up in Nievres, and in 1882, one was set up in Charolles. The books were merged in 1919, with the Nievres book assimilating the Charolais book.

In the 1930s, a Mexican industrialist, Jean Pugibet, who had learned about the Charolais cattle during his wartime service, imported a small herd to Mexico. In the late 1930s, some of Pugibet's Charolais cattle were purchased by private breeders in the United States, including the Texan King Ranch, which purchased two Charolais bulls named Neptune and Ortolan, and many cattle in the United States with Charolais ancestry go back to these two bulls. However, outbreaks of Foot and Mouth Disease in Mexico stopped further imports, causing a risk of too much inbreeding, and farmers could only cross-breed with other cattle. While this cross-breeding can strengthen the stock of other breeds, the purity of the Charolais breed became tainted.

Some Charolais were exported from France in small quantities after World War II from 1950-56, and by the 1960s, exports increased to hundreds of bulls and thousands of cows. Today, these cattle need to be 31/32 parts Charolais to be considered purebred, but cattle with less than 31/32 parts can be recorded and registered and then bred up to standard. It takes five generations to achieve this. With the importation of many French Charolais, the purity of the Charolais breed made an impressive come-back.

Charolais are easy-going, gentle and docile cattle with large, heavily muscled frames and long bodies. Males can weigh 2,200-3,600 lbs. and females 1500-2,600 lbs. They are typically a white-cream color with a pale muzzle and hooves. They are naturally horned, but some breeding practices up-breed them to be polled (without horns) for safety reasons. Mothers have good maternal instincts, and calves are born vigorous and healthy and gain weight quickly. While they are good draft animals and produce large quantities of milk, they are primarily bred for meat production. They have rugged hooves that allow for grazing on rough terrains that other breeds can't utilize. In winter and colder climates, they grow thicker and longer hair. But they do not do well in extreme temperatures, whether hot or cold.

Charolais cattle are now a world breed found in 68 countries, especially in the United States, Mexico, Australia, the UK and Europe. They are still often crossbred with other cattle to introduce hardiness and muscle. Their natural lifespan is 15-20 years.

DUCK

Duck (Mallard Duck) — *Anas platyrhynchos*

Besides being the most widespread and recognizable duck in the world, the mallard duck is also the ancestor of most domestic duck breeds. It is found throughout North America, Eurasia, and North Africa and has been introduced in Australia, New Zealand and South America. It prefers a habitat with lakes, ponds, or wetlands and is commonly seen in urban and suburban parks. These ducks can migrate many miles to southern, warmer climates in the winter if there is insufficient food.

The mallard is a large duck, about 20-26 in. long and weighs about 2-3 lbs. They have rounded heads, flat wide bills, and webbed feet. The males have a distinctive dark iridescent green head with a white neck ring, yellow bill, brown chest and wings with white-edged blue speculum patches, grayish-white body and black rear feathers. In contrast, the females and juveniles have a neutral, mottled brown plumage that gives them well-camouflaged protection. These ducks are dabbling ducks, which means they don't dive but tip their tail up when they search for food under water. They eat vegetation as well as small prey such as insects, worms, and freshwater shrimp. They are social and like to be in large flocks. They are also strong fliers, and migrating flocks can go as fast as 55 mph. While female mallards make a loud quack sound, the male makes a quieter rasping sound.

Mallard ducks pair in the fall, court during the winter and are generally monogamous for the length of the breeding season. The male can mate with other females as well (a common practice among birds that is called extra-pair copulation). The pair looks for a site together and prefers a secluded area near water with protective vegetation that can be used to hide or cover the nest. The female digs a shallow hole in the ground, which she lines with vegetation and down feathers from her breast. The mother lays 1-2 eggs at a time, and the clutch can be large, 5-15 eggs, a quantity that helps mitigate the high mortality rate among young ducklings.

Interestingly, while the eggs are laid at different times, they all hatch at about the same time. The male sticks around and protects the female as she lays her eggs, but once the eggs are laid, the male's job is done, and he will leave to join other males. Only the female will incubate the eggs and take care of the young. The ducklings hatch covered in down in about 28 days and are precocial, meaning they can walk and swim almost immediately after hatching. It will take about 60 days before they can fly.

After breeding, both sexes molt or shed all of their flight feathers and are flightless for about a month and more vulnerable to predators. The male's colorful feathers are replaced with dull camouflage feathers (called eclipse plumage) that help protect him. When the male is in eclipse plumage, both sexes look alike, but they are still distinguishable because the male has a yellow bill and the female has an orange bill. In the fall, he will regain his colorful feathers.

Mallard ducks have a long history and were raised for meat by the ancient Romans, Egyptians and Chinese. Today, they are a popular farmed duck for meat and eggs and also a popular game animal, but federal and wildlife agencies keep a close watch on the numbers. Mallard ducks have an IUCN rating of least concern, and their lifespan can be 5-10 years.

ELEPHANT

Elephant (African Elephant)   *Loxodonta africana and Loxodonta cyclotis*

There are two species of African elephants, the savanna or bush elephant (*L. africana*) and the smaller forest elephant (*L. cyclotis*). The savanna elephant is the largest land mammal in the world and weighs up to seven tons with a height of up to 12 ft. at the shoulder. It lives in savannas and grasslands in south and east Africa and in the Sahara and Namib deserts. The forest elephant has smoother and darker gray skin, weighs up to three tons with a height of up to 8.2 ft. and lives in dense west African forests. While the savanna elephant has wrinkly gray skin, large triangular ears and tusks that curve up and outward, the forest elephant has smoother and darker gray skin, rounder ears and straighter, downward tusks. In both species, the male is bigger than the female, and both sexes have tusks. They have peripheral vision, not binocular, and are nearsighted. Their feet have padding that helps them to walk more silently.

Both species have long, prehensile trunks that are used for breathing, moving food and water to the mouth, vocalizing, spraying water or dust, and even snorkeling to breathe air when underwater. They also use their trunks to socialize and often entwine their trunks when greeting each other. Their ears can serve as cooling fans when flapped. African elephants need little sleep, just a few hours in the early morning and at midday. They usually walk about four mph but can run for short distances, and are also good swimmers and can dog paddle. They smear mud on their skin and take dust baths to protect themselves from the sun and insects. They grow six sets of teeth (two molars up and two down) in their lifetime. Their vocalizations include high-pitched sounds as well as low-frequency infrasound (unheard by humans) that carry vast distances, enabling them to communicate with other elephants miles away. With their acute sense of smell, they can also smell an approaching rain shower miles away. They have very developed brains and are intelligent, with good memories that guide them along the same corridors as their ancestors during the changing seasons.

Female elephants are social and live in herds of 6-70, led by a matriarch (usually the oldest female). The herd consists of older cows, daughters, nieces and young males. The females develop strong bonds and spend their entire lives in the herd. The male will separate from the herd in adolescence (10-19 years) and go off on its own or join a smaller, loosely knit male herd that tends to stay near the matriarchal herd for socializing and mating.

There is no specific breeding season. The male reaches sexual maturity at 12-15 years, but he usually doesn't breed before his mid-thirties because he needs to gain the size and weight to compete with older males for mating rights. The adult male also goes into a period of musth once a year when he experiences heightened aggression, higher testosterone levels and more sexual activity. The female reaches sexual maturity at age 10-11. When a female goes into estrus, she emits chemicals in her urine and feces that attract males, and she may mate with more than one male. Gestation is 22 months, and usually, one calf is born, weighing up to 250 lbs. with a height of 3 ft. The mother leaves her herd to give birth, and when she returns with her offspring a few days later, the entire herd will gather to inspect the calf. Calves are very dependent on their mother's milk and will nurse for at least four years, but they also begin to eat vegetation a few months after birth. All female members of the herd will help care for the calves.

African elephants are considered a keystone species, meaning that they are vital to the entire ecosystem. They spend about 18 hours a day searching for food and eating hundreds of pounds of plant matter. Their migrations can be 15 or more miles a day, depending on food availability. They follow and create significant clearings and corridors, and that, along with their digging of waterholes, greatly benefits other animals. They also distribute plant and fruit seeds through their feces, which in turn provide nourishment to plants, animals and insects.

These elephants have a lifespan of about 70 years and have been observed to have rituals related to death. When a member dies, the entire herd appears to grieve and places grasses and branches on the body. They also may stay with the body for a number of days. The savanna elephant is considered endangered, and the forest elephant is critically endangered. They are threatened by poaching, human-wildlife conflict, and habitat loss. While nearly three-five million elephants existed in the early 20th century, today's population has dropped to a worrisome 400,000.

FOX

Fox (Arctic Fox, Polar Fox) *Vulpes lagopus*

The arctic fox, also called a polar fox, is an extremely hardy mammal that can withstand some of the harshest frigid temperatures on the planet, often way below 0°F in the winter. It is found in the circumpolar regions in North America and Eurasia. In North America, these regions include the tundras and pack ice in Alaska, northern Canada and the Arctic Archipelago.

The arctic fox is small, about 43 in. in length (including 15 in. tail) and weighs 6-10 lbs. With its dense fur, compact rounded body, fur-covered soles and bushy tail, it is well adapted to the arctic environment. In fact, it doesn't start shivering until temperatures fall below -90ºF. It accumulates body fat in the fall to help insulate itself. It has the unique ability to conserve energy by keeping its paw temperatures cooler than its warmer core temperature yet warm enough to keep its soles from freezing. When resting, the fox can wrap itself into a tight circle, with the tail covering its face like a blanket. If caught in a blizzard far from its den, it can burrow in the snow for protection.

Most arctic foxes have long, thick white fur during the winter and molt to shorter brown fur in the summer. A smaller number, usually in coastal rocky areas, has a light blue-grayish color that darkens in the summer. These fur colors provide good camouflage in the areas where they live. Arctic foxes live in family groups that usually consist of a male, two females (the male's mate and a nonbreeding female from last year's litter) and the litter. Their dens are dug 6-12 ft. below the ground surface in sandy, well-drained soil and have many tunnels and entrances to allow for predator evasion. Dens may be located on a mound in the tundra or under rocks at the base of a cliff, and entrances often face south for the warmth of the sun. Arctic foxes can dig new dens or use old dens that have been used by many generations of foxes over hundreds of years.

Arctic foxes can be active day or night and have a home range of 10-15 square miles but can travel much greater distances. They are nomadic and take frequent commuting trips in small bands for 2-3 days for hunting and scavenging. Some may migrate seaward in the fall and then inland in the spring, and others remain year-round residents. Arctic foxes are omnivorous and opportunistic eaters, and their diet includes lemmings, voles, eggs, fish, insects, berries and carrion. They can hear lemmings burrowing under the snow 4-5 in. deep and will pounce into the snow to catch them. In areas where the arctic fox is very dependent on the lemmings for food, its population size goes up and down cyclically with the lemming population. Foxes also travel on pack ice during winter, looking for seal carcasses left by polar bears, and they can smell a carcass many miles away. They cache extra food in their dens for later use.

The breeding season is April-May. Arctic foxes reach sexual maturity at 9-10 months and are monogamous for the season and often for life. Gestation is 52 days, and in the spring, the mother gives birth to about 5-8 pups in her den. Both parents feed and raise the pups, who are born with dark brown fur. Pups begin eating meat at one month and are fully weaned at one and a half months. They begin to hunt and range away from the den at three months. The father may mate with the mother about two weeks after the first litter is born to try for a second litter. The mortality of pups is high, and most won't make it beyond the first year. Families break up in the fall and live solitary lives in the winter except when gathering around to feed on a carcass.

Arctic foxes are valued for their dense coats. In the past, their population had been threatened by overhunting, but demand for pelts has diminished, and this is no longer a problem. The current number of pelts collected per year in Alaska averages about 4,000, which does not affect population levels and is important to the indigenous economy. Natural predators include wolves, polar bears and wolverines. Climate change, including the continuing disappearance of sea ice, threatens the arctic fox's future. Despite these issues, their IUCN rating is of least concern. The arctic fox can live 3-6 years in the wild.

GROUNDHOG

Groundhog (Woodchuck, Whistle Pig) *Marmota monax*

The groundhog, also known as a woodchuck, is a large ground squirrel found in North America from Alaska to the southern United States. It has a chubby, stocky build with large black eyes, four large incisors, thick long hair, short, strong legs, and long claws. It is an intelligent and curious animal and whistles to communicate danger, giving it the alternative name of whistle pig. Its habitat includes woodland edges, gardens, open fields and pastures. If food is plentiful, it keeps to a small home range of about 200 yards close to its burrow entrance.

The groundhog is built to dig and is an excellent burrowing architect. It builds an elaborate system of caves below the frost line about 2-6 ft. deep and as long as 24 ft., with some larger side chambers and as many as five entrances for predator evasion. The chambers are designated for living, hibernation or nursery, and there is even a space allotted for animal waste. While usually solitary and territorial, it will sometimes share a burrow with others. It also forms bonds with its offspring and spends time with family groups while foraging for food. It is mostly active during the day, feeding during early morning and late afternoon and staying close to its burrow for safety. There is usually a large mound of dirt remaining outside the main burrow entrance where the groundhog hangs out, standing erect to survey the land, watch for predators, or bask in the sun. Predators include bears, bobcats, coyotes, and badgers. If a predator is near, the groundhog will most likely jump into the safety of its burrow. It can also climb a tree or swim if necessary, or it can use its teeth and claws to protect itself. It can run up to ten mph. The groundhog experiences a true hibernation for as long as six months in colder climates to shorter periods in warmer climates. It gains weight in the summer to prepare for hibernation and can lose up to half its body weight during hibernation.

Mostly vegetarian, the groundhog eats grasses, plants, fruits, berries, vegetables, grasshoppers, grubs and small animals. While it can drink water when available, it usually gets enough water from plants that can also provide moisture from dew or rain. It eats about one and a half pounds of food a day. Not surprisingly, farmers and gardeners often consider the groundhog a pest. Besides plant and crop damage, their burrowed holes can cause broken legs to both humans and livestock, as well as damage to farm equipment.

Males are slightly larger than females. Depending on the location, breeding occurs from late February to late April, toward the end of hibernation, when the male leaves his burrow and searches to mate with females in their burrows. Although not monogamous, the male may remain with the female during gestation (32 days). The litter is usually 3-5 pups who are born blind and helpless. They are nursed by the mother, open their eyes at four weeks and are weaned at six weeks. They rely heavily on their mother for food, protection, and to learn survival skills. In the fall, the family group usually scatters, and the young begin burrowing on their own.

In folklore, groundhogs are thought to have the ability to forecast spring, and in the United States, there is an annual Groundhog Day on February 2 to celebrate this so-called ability. If the groundhog does not see its shadow, spring is close at hand, but if it sees its shadow, there are six more weeks of winter. Groundhogs are good for the environment. With all their burrowing, they help to mix and aerate the soil. Their abandoned burrows can be used by other animals like rabbits, skunks and foxes. Natural predators include coyotes, bobcats and large dogs. Groundhogs are also game animals, hunted for food and fur. Their IUCN rating is of least concern, and their lifespan in the wild is up to six years.

HIPPOPOTAMUS

Hippopotamus (Common Hippopotamus)   *Hippopotamus amphibius*

There are two species of hippopotamuses found in Africa today. The larger hippo, discussed here, often called the common hippopotamus, lives in Sub-Saharan Africa and the smaller pygmy hippo lives in the rain forests of West Africa. The word "hippopotamus" comes from the ancient Greek word for "river horse." The hippo is semi-aquatic, and water helps relieve and support its heavy weight. It prefers to live in slow-moving rivers and lakes or swamps that are close to grasslands.

The hippo is a very large, barrel-shaped animal about 7-16 ft. long, 4-5 ft. high at the shoulder, with a weight of up to 4 1/2 tons. Adapted well for water, its ears, eyes and nose are located on top of its head, allowing it to see, hear, and smell when almost totally submerged. It has short columnar legs and webbed toes. When totally underwater, its nostrils will close, and clear membranes will cover and serve as goggles for its eyes. It also has two large tusks in its jaw for defense and uses its tough lips to tear grass to eat. Hippos are loud and can vocalize both on land and under water.

Nocturnal, hippos spend up to 18 daytime hours resting and cooling in water. They hang out in herds of 20-100 or larger, led by a dominant male who is very territorial about his stretch of water from intruders and rival males, often scattering dung to mark territory in the water and on the banks. The herd consists of females with their calves and males who defer to the dominant male. When in water, females tend to be in the center of the pool and males on the outer edges and banks, protecting the herd.

When totally under water, adults need to surface every 4-6 minutes for air, and the young every 2-3 minutes. But the hippo can also sleep under water because it has a reflex that spurs it to rise up for air and sink down without waking. Hippos cannot swim and are too dense to float. Instead, they walk in slow motion on the riverbed and push up when they need to surface for air. Hippos have very thick, almost hairless skin that is vulnerable to sunburn and dehydration. The water helps, but the hippo also secretes a red mucous from its pores that acts as a sunscreen and may also serve as an antibiotic for any skin cuts.

Hippos are active at night, and when the sun goes down they let go of their herd behavior and leave the water individually to walk up to 2-3 miles on well-worn paths to nearby grasslands where they can graze and consume as much as 80 lbs. of grass per night. They do not exhibit territorial behavior on land, and they return to the river by daylight.

The breeding season is usually February-August but can be year-round. Both sexes reach sexual maturity at about 3 1/2 years. The dominant male has breeding rights to all the females in his herd, though sometimes he allows subservient males to breed. The male will submissively approach the females and sniff their posteriors to find a female in heat. He then pushes her out of the group and chases her into deeper waters. After some conflict between the two, he mounts her while pushing her head under water. Gestation is eight months, and most births are during the wettest time of the year. The mother will leave the herd for a week or so to give birth to one calf (50-120 lbs.) and bond with it before returning to the herd. The birth can be either on land or under water, in which case the mother may need to push the newborn calf up to the surface for air. The calf may ride on the mother's back in deep water. The calf is well adapted for nursing under water since it can close its nostrils, and it is weaned at about 18 months. It will usually stay with the mother for 7-8 years.

Hippos are good for the ecosystem. Their dung supplies nutrients to fish and invertebrates. Their well-worn paths can be used by other animals and also provide channels for water to flow and overflow during the rainy season, creating lagoons and side pools where small fish can take refuge during droughts. The hippo also opens its mouth wide occasionally for fish in the river to clean its teeth, which benefits all parties. Because of its size, aggressiveness and unpredictability, the hippo is one of the most dangerous animals in the world. It kills about 500 humans a year, often by capsizing boats that enter its territory. And since it can run 20 mph for short stretches, it can easily overtake a fleeing human. While the adult hippo is generally too large to be threatened by predators, its young can be vulnerable to crocodiles, lions, hyenas and leopards. The hippo is also threatened by poachers and habitat loss. Its IUCN rating is vulnerable, and its lifespan in the wild is 40-50 years.

IBIS

Ibis (White American Ibis) — *Eudocimus albus*

The ibis is a common wading bird in southeast Florida and the Caribbean Islands with a range that extends as far north as Virginia, then south to Florida and the coasts of Texas, and further south to the coasts of Mexico, Central America and northern South America. In Florida, the ibis is associated with hurricanes and has a reputation for being a courageous bird, the last to leave and first to return after hurricanes and storms. It feeds in shallow water (salt, brackish or fresh), and its habitat includes coastal marshes, wetlands, mangrove swamps and mudflats. The ibis is often a year-round resident, but some migrate in the winter to southern parts of its range. It has a foot-ball-shaped body, a reddish face with blue eyes, a reddish down-curved bill and long reddish legs. It has white plumage with black wing tips and weighs about 2 1/2 lbs. with a height of 2 ft. and a wingspan of 3 ft.

With safety in numbers, the ibis nests and feeds in colonies that can be as large as 500 or even in the thousands, including spoonbills, herons, and other wading birds. It spends most of its day looking for food and will fly up to 15 miles a day to search in different wetland sites as needed. It also likes to roost in trees near water, resting and preening feathers with its bill. While mostly a quiet bird, it can communicate with a honking sound. When flying in groups, ibises fly in V-shaped formations called skeins.

The ibis wades slowly in shallow water (less than 8 in.), sweeping its bill from side to side and probing the sediment for small prey, including small fish, crabs and crayfish. Its underwater prey are felt but not seen and are often swallowed whole. Alternatively, the ibis might stab or take the prey in its mouth and carry it elsewhere to rinse the mud off or remove the claws of crabs and crayfish before eating. Other wading birds often follow ibises to take advantage of the disturbed sediment and search for leftovers. When out of the water, the ibis locates small land prey by sight.

The male ibis is larger than the female. Both sexes reach sexual maturity at three years, and breeding is in the spring. The male's courtship displays include head shaking, preening and up-and-down spiraling flights to show off with other males near the colony. When the male chooses a mate, he grabs and shakes her head. The pair will continue to bond, greet each other with sticks, cross their necks, and preen each other.

Ibises are monogamous during the breeding season, but the male may also mate with other females (a practice among birds called extra-pair copulation). The female chooses the nest site, often located on the fork of a tree or in a shrub near water. If high nesting sites are not available, the nest may be built on a clump of grass. Both the male and female build the nest together, and the male defends the nest and partner from rival males and predators. The female lays 3-5 eggs, and both sexes incubate the eggs (21 days). The chicks are born helpless with eyes closed and covered with black and gray down. Their bills are straight and begin to curve at two weeks. Both parents care for the chicks until they are ready to leave the nest in 40-60 days. The parents tend to forage for food in fresh water sites because the chicks cannot yet tolerate salt water. Juveniles have brown upper feathers, white lower feathers, and a streaky neck, and they become more splotchy brown and white as they shift to adult plumage.

Ibises benefit the ecosystem because they disperse nutrients when carrying prey from the water to their nesting sites. They are detrimental to crayfish farmers in Louisiana, who may resort to hunting them to protect their stock. Ibises are also vulnerable to egg predation from many small animals, especially the fish crow. While threatened by coastal development and habitat loss, the ibis population remains stable and of least concern, and their lifespan is up to 16 years in the wild.

JAVELINA

Javelina (Collared Peccary, Skunk Pig) *Dicotyles tajacu*

The javelina, also called a "collared peccary," is a New World species, and its core group inhabits rain forests in South and Central America. It is a relative newcomer to the United States and thought to have migrated to the southwest early in the 20th century, which is now its northernmost range. Javelinas look a lot like the Old World pig species. Among the differences between the two species, javelinas have straight tusks and small round ears and pigs have curved tusks and large upright ears.

In the United States, javelinas live in desert environments that include palo verde forests and arid grasslands with shrubs and cacti, often near a water source. They can also be found on agricultural land and in urban areas. They live in family groups or herds (squadrons) of 6-12 and sometimes as many as 50. Each herd is led by an alpha male, usually the largest male, who has to compete constantly to maintain his dominant status. The javelina is highly social and well-integrated into its herd and likely could not survive without it. The herd offers group protection, and members will join together to ward off predators. Each herd needs a territory of 75-700 acres with access to water, food and shelter. While territories may overlap, herds avoid occupying a shared territory at the same time.

The javelina is medium-sized and weighs 35-55 lbs. with a height of up to 24 in. at the shoulder and a length of 3-4 ft. It has a large head, long snout, and coarse salt-and-pepper hair that forms a lighter "collar" around the shoulders. It also has a mane of long, stiff hair along its back that stands up when threatened. Sometimes called skunk pigs, javelinas have a scent gland above their tail, which they use to mark their territory by rubbing rocks, stumps and trunks. Members of the herd also mark each other with a scent so that they can readily recognize each other despite their poor vision. The javelina also makes various vocalizations to communicate with the herd. When threatened, it makes a barking alarm sound along with a chattering sound with its tusks, inciting the herd to run fast in all directions.

The javelina is mostly herbivorous and eats agaves, green vegetation, seeds, fruit and cacti, but also insects and reptiles. Succulents provide needed moisture when not near a water source, and they get most of their moisture from the prickly pear, thorns and all. Herds travel about a mile each day in search of food. In the summer, javelinas will leave their sleeping area (often in caves, overhangs or dense thickets) at night to feed. In the winter, they are more active and feed in the early morning, late afternoon, and at night. They prefer being near a permanent water source for both water intake and wallowing in the mud. They are unable to cool off by panting but will lie down and rest in the shade during the heat of the day.

The male is slightly larger than the female and has longer tusks. Males reach sexual maturity at 11 months and females at 8-14 months. Breeding can be any time of the year, and the alpha male has exclusive breeding rights. Gestation is about 150 days, and the mother can have 1-5 young who weigh about a pound apiece. The mother separates from the herd before giving birth, and the precocial newborns are able to walk with the mother back to the herd just one day after birth. The mother is fiercely protective of her babies, especially from males who have been known to kill newborns in order to mate with the mother. Only older females in the herd are allowed to get close to them. The babies nurse for eight weeks, after which they begin to eat solid food. Babies have red to brown hair and are called "reds" until they acquire adult coloration at three months, and they stay close to the mother during the first year. Javelinas do not form long-term pairs.

The javelina is hunted for food and its hide, as well as by farmers to protect crops, and it has become a big game animal in Arizona and Texas. The adult javelina can fend off most natural predators such as mountain lions, bobcats and coyotes, but the young have a high mortality rate due to predation, weather and hunger. The javelina is shy and rarely attacks a human unless it feels threatened. It can, however, viciously attack dogs (and humans walking dogs) because, with poor eyesight, it can mistake a dog for a coyote. Despite hunting and predation, the javelina species is stable, and its IUCN rating is of least concern. The javelina's lifespan is ten years in the wild.

KOALA

Koala   *Phascolarctos cinereus*

The koala is native to eastern and southern Australia and is one of Australia's most recognizable animals. It is arboreal and lives in eucalyptus forests and woodlands. The koala's diet consists mostly of eucalyptus leaves, which have a high water content, so koalas generally don't need to drink water. The name "koala" in fact evolved from the aboriginal word "gula," which means "no water." The koala came close to extinction in the early 20th century due to fires and extensive hunting for its rich fur coat. Since 1927, it has been protected by law from hunting.

The koala is a stocky animal about 2-3 ft. high and up to 33 lbs. with gray to brown fur on its back, white fur on the front and no tail. It has a large head, big ears, small eyes and a black nose. The koala has strong limbs, opposable thumbs on its front paws, as well as sharp claws on all four paws, making it well adapted to climbing. The back paws have two fused digits that can be used for grooming. Koalas also have good hearing and a good sense of smell and are able to swim. Their digestive system has uniquely adapted so that it can process eucalyptus leaves that are otherwise very poisonous. The koala can smell the toxicity levels in eucalyptus leaves, and while there are hundreds of different eucalyptus species in Australia, it eats only about five kinds. Because eucalyptus leaves contain very little nutrition and take a lot of energy to digest, the koala conserves energy by sleeping 18-20 hours/day and moving slowly. Also, the koala's brain is very small, which is thought to be an adaptation to the limits of its very slow metabolism.

Koalas are solitary, nocturnal animals and live in home ranges that overlap with each other. A home range is usually about 2-4 acres but can be larger or smaller depending on food availability. It must contain a sufficient number of food trees that the koala can regularly visit. The koala is nonmigratory and usually lives in its home range for its entire life. It spends most of its time high up in eucalyptus trees, where it is safe from predators and free to nap and feed on eucalyptus leaves. Built to be arboreal, the koala has an awkward gait on the ground, where it spends little time. But at night, it can climb down (backward) to the ground to move to another tree as needed. It communicates with vocalizations like bellows, snarls and screams.

Koalas are very territorial and do not interact with each other except when defending territory or mating. Both sexes mark territory with urine, and males also use a dark brown scent gland located on their chests. The scent can be strong enough after a koala dies to discourage any other koala from moving in until it wears off in about a year. The only bonding relationships between koalas are between the mother and her offspring.

Koalas are marsupials, i.e., females have pouches. Males are about 50% larger than females. During the breeding season (September- February), the dominant male (usually the biggest) makes bellowing sounds at night. He moves from tree to tree, searching to mate with females in estrus. Gestation takes 35 days, and the underdeveloped newborn (usually just one), about the size of a honey bee, leaves the birth canal, makes its way to the mother's pouch through a side opening and attaches itself to one of two teats. The pouch opening has a sphincter muscle that keeps the baby secure while it nurses for 6-7 months. At about 22 weeks, the baby or joey opens its eyes and begins to lean out of the pouch to feed on "pap," a specialized form of runny feces from the mother that contains predigested and detoxified eucalyptus leaves as well as a special gut bacteria that the joey vitally needs in order to gain the ability to process eucalyptus leaves on its own. At seven months, the joey leaves the pouch and is carried on the mother's back while it begins to eat its own leaves. At one year, it is independent and will leave to find a home range of its own. Young males can have difficulty finding a home range because of hostile males who try to keep them away. They may need to live a nomadic lifestyle on the periphery of home ranges before finally finding their own space.

The koala's natural predators include dingos and large pythons, and the young are vulnerable to large birds of prey. However, the koala is more threatened by cars and habitat loss due to agriculture and urbanization. About 80% of its habitat has disappeared since the European settlement in the late 18th century. The koala is also vulnerable to wild fires since eucalyptus trees are very flammable and koalas move very slowly. Its IUCN rating is endangered, and its lifespan in the wild is about 10-13 years.

LYNX

Lynx (Canada Lynx) *Lynx canadensis*

The Canada lynx lives mostly in Alaska and Canada, but some are found in parts of the northern United States. Its habitat includes mature, dense forests with undergrowth, rocky areas and tundras. The lynx is a secretive, quiet animal and is rarely seen in the wild. It has a poor sense of smell but excellent hearing and vision. Because of its acute vision, the lynx has a reputation in folklore for being a keeper of secrets, clairvoyant and seeing what others cannot.

The lynx can be 19-22 in. tall at the shoulder, 26-42 in. long and weighs 18-40 lbs. Its hind legs are longer, so its back slants downward toward the front. Its thick winter fur is grayish and slightly mottled, especially long at the neck, providing very good insulation in subzero temperatures. It has black tufted ear tips, a stubby black-tipped tail, and large snowshoe-like padded paws well adapted for walking on snow.

Lynxes are nocturnal, solitary and territorial. They roam about six miles a day on home ranges that vary widely from 5-100 square miles, depending on food availability. Lynxes mark their territories with urine and feces and avoid each other except during the breeding season. The female's home range can overlap with other females' home ranges. The male's home range is separate from other males' home ranges but usually includes several female home ranges, and it is thought that they are polygynous. Lynxes are active year-round, though they may bed in the insulation of snow when the temperatures are especially harsh. They shelter in natural settings like rock crevices, under logs or branches, or under a rock ledge or shrubs. Lynxes can climb trees to escape predators or to rest, and they can also swim.

Lynxes are carnivores and eat birds, fish, mammals and carrion. They can kill prey as large as a deer that has been weakened in winter. When hunting, they quietly track their prey until within range and then pounce. They can also spend hours in hiding, waiting in ambush along a trail used by snow shoe hares and then pounce when one arrives. They prefer hunting in forests but will move to tundras and above the tree line when food is scarce. The snowshoe hare comprises 70% or more of the lynx's diet, and the lynx is so dependent on the snowshoe hare that its population goes dramatically up and down with the snowshoe hare population in about 10-year cycles. In effect, this cyclical synchronization between the two species keeps the populations of both species in balance.

The male lynx is slightly larger than the female. The female reaches sexual maturity at ten months but often waits another year to breed, and the male at 2 to 3 years. The female goes into estrus once a year in January-February, and it is only during the breeding season that lynxes may travel in pairs. Gestation is 8-10 weeks, and the litter size is usually 2-4 kittens. Newborns are born helpless with eyes closed and a full coat of fluffy hair, weighing close to 1/2 lb. They open their eyes at one month and nurse for five months when they start eating prey. The male does no parenting, and the mother alone cares for and teaches survival skills to her kittens. This might include cooperative hunting, where the mother and kittens spread in a line to walk across an open area, and when one flushes out a prey, it can be caught by another. The young stay with their mother until the next breeding season. They molt to their adult coat at 8-10 months and are independent at 10 months. The young are vulnerable to starvation, especially when the population of snowshoe hares is at its low cycle.

Natural predators are wolves and coyotes. Lynxes help the ecosystem by hunting snowshoe hares and voles, which are considered pests. Since the 17th century, they have been trapped for their fur, but hunting is now regulated with seasons and quotas. With logging, development and climate change, lynxes are vulnerable to habitat loss and need to migrate north to colder temperatures. Despite these issues, the IUCN rating for the species is of least concern, and they can live as long as 14 1/2 years in the wild.

MULE

Mule   *Equus mulus*

The mule is a cross between a male donkey and a female horse and is the oldest and most commonly known hybrid, combining the best traits of the horse (speed and agility) with the donkey (intelligence, sure-footedness, cautiousness and endurance). A male horse and a female donkey can also be hybridized to create a hinny, but due to their physiology, it is impractical and rare. The mule can be either male or female, but with its genetic makeup, it is almost always sterile. Male mules need to be castrated to make them manageable and safe to handle. Mules have good memories, and it is thought that they don't forget bad treatment or bad handlers.

Mules are usually brown or gray, larger than a donkey and smaller than a horse but stouter, with long ears and a head that resembles a donkey. They are 50-70 in. tall at the withers with a weight of 600-1500 lbs. They can bray and whinny like their parents. The mule eats grass and hay, adapts to almost all climates and is found throughout the world. The common expression "as stubborn as a mule" is not necessarily a criticism but recognizes that a mule is intelligent and will not put itself in a dangerous situation.

Mules were first intentionally bred in ancient times in what are now parts of modern-day Turkey, and they were used as early as 3000 BCE in Egypt for carrying supplies, pulling wagons and farming. They were also used in ancient Rome and ancient Greece. The Roman military brought the mule across the Alps to Central Europe in the first century BCE. The breeding of mule hybrids eventually became a prosperous trade in Europe in the 18th century.

While Christopher Columbus brought donkeys and horses across the Atlantic in 1495 to breed mules for use in Central America, it was George Washington who became known as the first breeder of mules in the United States. After the Revolutionary War, Washington returned to his farm in Mt. Vernon, Virginia. He recognized the valuable impact the mule could make in agricultural use, and for a number of years he worked to secure a larger and stronger breeding donkey than what was currently available in the United States. In 1785, he was gifted by King Charles III in Spain with two female donkeys (jennies) and one male donkey (jack) from the famed Andalusian stock. A year later, Washington's friend Marquise de Lafayette gifted him with several Maltese jennies and one jack. Washington then bred a Maltese jack with an Andalusian jenny, resulting in an exceptional breeding jack that he named Compound. Compound was used for stud services and to sire a superior stock of donkeys called the American Mammoth Jackstock. Washington also hybridized Compound and the newly bred jacks with his horses, and in less than 15 years, he had about 58 mules on his farm. These bigger and stronger mules changed the face of southern agriculture as they became the preferred draft animal over horses and oxen in the South.

Mules grew from a zero population in 1785 to 855,000 in the United States in 1808. A farmer and two mules could easily plow 16 acres a day. Mules on wagon trains going west could cover more mileage per day than horses or oxen. Jacks continued to be imported in large numbers from Spain in the mid-1880s, and by the end of the century, the mule population had grown to over 4 million due to the cotton boom. Mules were also used in mule trains, such as the 20-mule teams in the 1890s that hauled over 36 tons of borax from Death Valley to Mojave, California. Mules have been used in large numbers to transport supplies in many wars from antiquity up to the 20th century, including World Wars I and II and the Vietnam War. U.S. Army mules could carry 20% of their weight for 15-20 miles per day. Because of their sure-footedness and strong hooves, mules were invaluable on treacherous, rocky paths where a vehicle could not go.

With the invention of the internal combustion engine and the subsequent availability of affordable tractors for small-scale farmers in the 1920s, the demand for mules dropped dramatically and permanently. The population of mules in the United States has dwindled down to about 200,000. Mules are now used on a much smaller scale for work and recreation. Being a hybrid animal, the mule is almost always under human care, and its IUCN rating is of least concern. Their lifespan is usually 30-40 years, but some can live as long as 50 years.

NUTHATCH

Nuthatch (Red-Breasted Nuthatch, Upside-Down Bird) *Sitta canadensis*

The red-breasted nuthatch is one of many species of nuthatches in the world. It is found throughout North America in Alaska, Canada and the northeastern and western United States. Its habitat includes spruce-fir and other coniferous and mixed forests. Like all nuthatches, it is called an "upside-down bird" because of its unique, energetic meanderings upside down and in all directions without any sense of "up" as it forages for insects on tree trunks and branches. They are usually year-round residents in their habitat, but some may migrate southward if food is scarce or if the weather is severe.

The red-breasted nuthatch is a small song bird about 4-6 inches long with a large head, white throat and face with a black cap bordered by white eyebrow lines above black eye lines. It has almost no neck and short legs, as well as a short tail. Its feet have three front toes and one large back toe, all with strong curved claws, so it does not need to use its tail for support, and it is well adapted for gravity-defying climbs. Females and juveniles are similar in markings but paler.

Red-breasted nuthatches are diurnal and spend their days foraging for insects and seeds on conifer tree trunks and branches. In their downward climb, they find insects that upward-climbing birds miss. They forage quickly, walking on the underside of branches and moving from tree to tree in short, bouncy flights. They travel through trees with chickadees, woodpeckers and kinglets. These nuthatches have an especially close relationship with black-capped chickadees and can recognize and respond to chickadee vocal messages that go beyond the usual alarm calls. The red-breasted nuthatch's vocalizations advertise their territory, and the sounds they make are high-pitched and nasal, like nya-nya or yank-yank.

The nuthatch is omnivorous and eats conifer seeds, insects and larvae. While it eats insects mostly from trees, it is also capable of catching insects in flight. It eats more insects in the summer and more conifer seeds in the winter. It also feeds on offerings like chopped nuts, seeds and suet from bird feeders. To open a hard nut or seed, it can wedge it into a bark crevice and hack it open. It caches collected food throughout its territory in bark crevices, in the ground or under stones for later use, which can help it survive during winter food shortages.

Both sexes reach sexual maturity at one year, and breeding occurs once a year in the spring. The male may court the female with a swaying, singing display with head up, wings down and fluffed back feathers, and he may also bring food to her. Pairs are monogamous during the breeding season and will often stay together through the next winter. While they can use an existing tree hole for a nest, they usually excavate a new cavity in dead or decaying trees. During the nest-building, they can be aggressive and territorial to keep other birds away. They line the cavity with soft materials, and both sexes will collect pitch in their bills to smear on both sides of the cavity entrance. Or they can carry pitch on a piece of bark, which they can use as an applicator. The pitch is thought to deter predators, and the pair will continue to apply the pitch as needed. The female lays 4-7 eggs, and incubation takes 12 days. The young are born helpless and are brooded by the mother but fed by both parents for 2-3 weeks before fledging, and they will often remain with the parents as a family for several more weeks.

Red-breasted nuthatches help the ecosystem by dispersing seeds and keeping insects under control. In western fruit orchards, they benefit pear orchards by eating an insect pest, Pear Psylla. Predators include sharp-shinned hawks, Cooper's hawks, spotted owls and weasels. In more developed areas, they can be prey to domestic cats, and the mortality rate can increase due to collisions with glass windows and buildings. Their IUCN rating is of least concern, and their lifespan in the wild is about six years.

OPOSSUM

Opossum (Virginia Opossum) *Didelphis virginiana*

Because the Virginia opossum shares many traits with the earliest marsupials (from 130 million years ago), it is often considered a living fossil. It is endemic to the Americas and is the only opossum as well as the only marsupial in the United States and Canada. It has a wide range in the United States and Central America. In the United States, the opossum is found east of the Rockies and on the west coast. Its range extends as far north as southern Ontario and south to Mexico and Central America. It needs to live in warmer climates because it is vulnerable to frostbite. Its habitat includes deciduous forests, open woods and farmland, preferably near sources of water. It also lives in developed areas near humans. The opossum's home range is about 30-95 acres, and it usually lives in its home range for its entire life. Opossums do not hibernate but are less active in winter and spend more time in shelter.

The opossum is about 13-22 in. long with a prehensile tail about 10-21 in. and weighs 4-15 lbs. It is grayish with a white triangular face and black eyes, black ears and a pointed nose. It has pink hairless feet and a pink hairless tail. Its front feet have five clawed toes, and its hind feet have four clawed toes and an opposable thumb. Opossums rarely get rabies and are resistant to snake venom.

The opossum is nocturnal and has good hearing and eyesight, as well as a keen sense of smell. It is terrestrial but well adapted to climbing and spends a lot of time in trees. It is nomadic within its home range and will move when food is scarce. It has a characteristic slow, hobbled walk. It looks for ready-made dry and dark shelters that include abandoned burrows, wood piles, rock crevices, caves, barns and under houses. It collects nesting materials of dry leaves, grass, twigs, plastic bags or fabric and uses its tail to carry it all to the shelter. The opossum usually has several active shelters so that it can move around and evade predators.

In facing a predator, the opossum can bare its teeth and growl, climb up a tree or jump into water and swim away. If all else fails, it has a unique involuntary response called "playing dead," where it stiffens into a catatonic state, falls on its side with teeth bared and tongue out, and emits a smelly fluid from its anal glands to deter the predator. It can remain in this state from a few minutes to six hours.

While insects are their main diet, opossums are opportunistic omnivores and eat eggs, fruit, frogs, snakes and carrion, and they are common predators of poultry farms. With 50 teeth in their mouth, they can eat bones for calcium, and with their opposable thumbs, they can forage through trash cans.

Males are slightly larger and have a musky scent gland on their chest. They also have larger home ranges and are polygynous. Females reach sexual maturity at 6 months and males at 8 months. Females have a 28-day estrus cycle and can have 1-3 liters per year. In the north, the breeding season is February-September, and the male attracts the female with clicking sounds. Gestation is 12-13 days. The litter size can be up to 20, and the underdeveloped newborns (joeys), about the size of a honey bee, will attempt to crawl to the mother's pouch, which is scented to guide them. However, many will die, unable to reach her pouch or attach to one of her 13 teats, so the mother averages about eight pouch-young per litter. The successful joeys nurse for about two months until they start opening their eyes and leave the pouch for their mother's back (holding on with their tails), and they begin to learn survival skills from the mother. They start eating solid food at 85 days and are fully weaned and independent at 93-105 days. Most joeys will then begin their solitary lives, but some will stay in the den with the mother a while longer. Males provide no parental care. Mortality of the young is high, and about 60% of joeys that leave the pouch will not survive to adulthood.

Opossums are hunted for their pelts and meat, which is thought to have medicinal benefits for ailments such as inflammation, gastritis and skin infections. The opossum's predators include dogs, coyotes, bobcats, and birds of prey, and many are killed by cars. Opossums benefit the ecosystem by dispersing seeds and cleaning up the environment by eating insects, cockroaches, rats, mice, carrion and rotting plant matter. Their IUCN rating is of least concern, and their lifespan is 1-2 years.

PIKA

Pika (American Pika, Rock Rabbit)   *Ochotona princeps*

The American pika is one of over 30 species of pikas in the world. It is thought to be of Siberian ancestry, crossing the former Bering land bridge from Asia to Alaska many thousands of years ago. Today, it is found in high alpine regions of western North America, as far north as BC and as far south as New Mexico. Like hares and rabbits, the pika belongs to the Lagomorpha order.

Despite its small stature and indisputable cuteness, the pika is a very tough and hardy animal that lives in inhospitable mountainous areas above the tree line. Also called a rock rabbit, its usual habitat is on rocky slopes with patches of vegetation or nearby meadows. The pika lives in large colonies and shares the burden of watching for predators and alerting with its high-pitched and squeaky alarm calls. But it is solitary, asocial and very territorial and marks its home range, up to a half-acre, with urine, feces and secretions from its cheek glands. Pikas find and modify appropriate spaces in rock piles or slides to use for dens. They do not hibernate but stay in their den for longer periods in the winter. They also don't burrow but can tunnel through snow to access food in nearby meadows.

Pikas have small round bodies about 7-8 in. long with no visible tail. They have thick gray fur, a white underside and dark round ears edged in white. Their paws and soles are densely furred, with five toes on the front paws and four on the back. Pikas are diurnal and most active in the early mornings and early evenings. They vocalize to advertise and protect their range, to warn of predators and to attract mates. Alarm calls are less frequently made for small predators like weasels, who are small enough to chase the pika into the rock crevices where its den is located. Pikas are herbivores and make hundreds of foraging trips daily, collecting wildflowers, grasses and other vegetation, which they eat on-site or carry back to collect in large drying piles (haystacks) near their dens. They mark their haystacks and fiercely guard them from other pikas who might steal them. Once the haystacks are dry, the pikas will cache them in their dens.

Because its diet contains a lot of cellulose, which is difficult to digest, the pika needs to ingest its food twice to get sufficient nutrition, a process called coprophagy. The vegetation they eat is processed in the caecum (between small and large intestines), where caecal pellets are formed. In contrast to the pika's hard fecal pellets, the caecal pellets are soft and provide more energy than the pika's stored plants. When the pika eliminates the caecal pellets, it will eat or cache them immediately. Pikas drink water if available but get most of the moisture they need from the vegetation they eat.

The male pika is slightly larger, and both sexes reach sexual maturity in about a year. The breeding season begins a month before the snow melts, and the male expands its territory to include a few females. Two pikas in adjacent territories will call to each other, starting the breeding process. If two males show up, the female can choose. Pikas are monogamous. Females are reflex ovulators, meaning they ovulate after mating, and they breed a second time after the first litter is born. Gestation is 30 days, and the average litter size is three pups. Pups are born about the size of a walnut, blind with little hair, and completely dependent on the mother. The mother continues to forage but also nurses the pups every few hours. The pups are weaned at four weeks when they are ready to leave the mother. Juveniles must find their own vacant territory and sometimes need to live on the fringes of multiple territories until a vacant spot opens up. If the population is saturated, some juveniles may die before finding a spot.

Predators include eagles, hawks, bobcats, foxes and weasels, and the pika's habitat is shrinking due to climate change. They cannot tolerate temperatures above 80º F and are an important indicator species for global warming. If their alpine habitat gets too warm, they are essentially stuck with nowhere to go. They are too vulnerable to both heat and predators to go below the tree line in search of another alpine habitat. It is against the law to hunt pikas. Despite habitat loss, the American pika's IUCN rating is of least concern, and its lifespan is 3-6 years.

QUAIL

Quail (Gambel's Quail) *Callipepla gambelii*

The Gambel's quail is found in desert regions in the southwestern United States, especially Arizona, but its range also extends to Mexico, Texas, New Mexico, California and southern parts of Utah, Nevada and Colorado. Its habitat includes desert plains with brushy and diverse vegetation, mesquite-lined river valleys, mountain foothills, and irrigation ditches in agricultural areas. It is also a common backyard bird in suburban settings. It needs a habitat that offers sufficient dense vegetation and trees so it can find shade as well as protection from predators.

A ground-dwelling bird, the Gambel's quail has a chunky roundish body 11-12 in. long and a top knot on its head. It has gray plumage with scaly feathers on the underside and a white chest, chestnut sides, and olive wings. Males have a more striking plumage with a larger top knot, black face and neck with rusty head cap and black belly patch.

Gambel's quails are nonmigratory and can fly only in short spurts. For most of the year, they hang out in family groups (coveys) of 16-20.

In the winter, families often combine with other coveys (40-50 birds). They are not territorial, and coveys travel and feed on each other's home ranges, which can be 20-94 acres. They communicate with varied calls and vocalizations as they walk slowly along the ground, foraging for food during mornings and late afternoons. During the heat of the day, they rest under the shade and protection of vegetation.

The Gambel's quail's diet includes mostly plants and seeds with some fruits, berries and insects during the breeding season. The young eat insects for protein but will switch to plants and seeds as they mature. While quails can get water from the vegetation they eat, they like to live near a water source. Because the quail's colors provide good camouflage, they may elect to remain motionless when threatened and hide in plain sight. They are fast runners, so they can also sprint for cover into brushy vegetation. At night, the covey roosts together either in low, dense trees or in low, heavy vegetation to avoid predators and get protection from the wind. Both sexes reach sexual maturity at one year, and females usually have one clutch a season. Breeding season is March through July when quails separate from the covey to mate. Males leave the covey first and look for females. The male courts the female by strutting, bowing and offering bits of food, a practice called tidbitting. Mating pairs become territorial and aggressive toward other pairs. The pair is monogamous for the season, but the female will sometimes abandon her mate and their brood and pair with another male. In this case, the abandoned male will take over parenting duties for their brood. Females select the nest site, occasionally on a suitable branch but more often on the ground or at the base of a rock or tree under protective vegetation. The pair will scrape a shallow bowl in the ground and line it with twigs, grass and feathers. The clutch size is 10-12 eggs, and incubation takes 22-23 days. Usually, the female incubates the eggs.

Interestingly, all eggs, whether laid sooner or later, hatch at the same time, called synchronized hatching. Just before hatching time, the mother calls out to the unhatched chicks, who cheep in response and cut small circular doors on the eggs (hinged with membrane) to open and hatch out. Both parents take care of the young, and the precocial chicks can follow their parents and feed themselves very soon after hatching. When the breeding season ends, the pair loses its territorial behavior and regroups into coveys. They practice mixed parenting, in which adults in the covey keep a protective eye on the chicks as they forage together.

Rain and temperature play a role in the quail's population level. If winter and spring provide heavy rain and cooler temperatures, the population goes up, and in the case of below-average rain and above-average temperatures, the population goes down. Nests at ground level are often raided for eggs by snakes and Gila monsters. Larger predators include bobcats, foxes, and coyotes. Quails are a popular game bird, hunted for meat, but hunting does not appear to affect the overall population. Because of the Gambel's quail's characteristics of socialization, monogamy, mixed parenting and vocalizing, they are considered to be very intelligent. While their habitat shrinks with development, they seem to do well in cultivated areas, and their population numbers remain stable. Their IUCN rating is of least concern, and their lifespan is 1 1/2 to 2 years.

RABBIT

Rabbit (Eastern Cottontail Rabbit)   *Sylvilagus floridanus*

The eastern cottontail is the most common rabbit species in North America. It is found in southern Canada, through the eastern two-thirds of the United States and south through eastern Mexico, Central America and northern South America. It has also been introduced to some parts of the northwest United States. Historically, the eastern cottontail's habitat increased in the United States as settlers cleared land. It seeks open grassy areas that have some kind of escape cover, such as edge environments with fields bordered by woodlands or brush. In urban areas, lawns with shrubbery make a good habitat.

The eastern cottontail has long ears and large brown eyes, reddish-brown to gray fur with a white underside, muscular hind quarters with large hind feet and a short fluffy tail that is white underneath. It is 15-19 in. long and weighs about 2 1/2 lbs. It has a keen sense of sight, smell and hearing. It has a small blind spot in front of its nose but can see almost 360º.

Active year-round from dusk until dawn, eastern cottontails do not hibernate. Their home range is 1-2 acres but can be larger or smaller depending on season, terrain and food resources. They are solitary, tend to be intolerant of each other and usually live in their home range for their entire life. During the day, the eastern cottontail keeps hidden in places like an abandoned burrow or a shallow depression in a thicket or in a hollow under a log. It can sit still for hours at a time, resting and grooming itself. Sometimes, it will get up on its hind legs to survey for predators. It communicates with grunts, distress cries, and thumping its hind legs. If faced with a predator, it has escape strategies that include freezing in the hope it won't be noticed or flushing, where it quickly flees in a zig-zag pattern for cover. It can also slink down, quietly moving close to the ground with its ears laid back. Unfortunately for the eastern cottontail, it is at the bottom of the food chain and an important source of food for many animals. If caught, it is easy prey and usually does not fight its predator.

Opportunistic herbivores, eastern cottontails eat various grasses, bark, garden produce and farm crops with a preference for tender young shoots, clover, dandelions and tulips. They can't fully digest the vegetation they eat, so they need to redigest their food in order to get vital nutrients, a process called coprophagy. Some of the cottontail's fecal waste is processed in the caecum (between small and large intestines), forming green and moist pellets that contain undigested, nutritious vegetation. These caecal pellets are soft compared to their hard fecal pellets. When the cottontail eliminates the caecal pellets, it will swallow them whole, and the redigestion begins.

The breeding season is from mid-February to September but can vary widely by location. Eastern cottontails reach sexual maturity at three months. They are promiscuous and mate with no lasting bond. Males fight each other to establish dominance and mating priority. Males and females may perform an odd mating dance in which the male chases the female until she stops and boxes him with her front paws. Then they crouch facing each other and alternate jumping two feet straight up in the air for a while before mating. Gestation is about 28 days. The female picks a nest site with some cover, such as in a hollow under a shrub or log or in tall grass. She scrapes a shallow nest in the ground with her front paws and lines it with grass, twigs, and fur pulled from her chest and belly. The litter size averages five, and the babies (kits) are about two inches long with fine hair, blind, deaf and totally dependent on the mother. The mother does not stay with the kits but rests in her own spot about 20' away and returns to nurse them about 2-3 times at night. The kits grow quickly, open their eyes in a week and take short trips away from the nest at two weeks to eat grass. They are completely weaned at four to five weeks and fully independent at seven weeks when they disperse. Males play no role in parenting. Newborn mortality is high, however, and nearly half the kits will die within a month from birth. The mother can mate again right after she gives birth and can have 3-4 litters in a season.

The eastern cottontail's predators include hawks, owls, red foxes and coyotes. It is often killed in car accidents, especially in the spring when it feeds on roadside grasses. It is also a popular game animal, hunted for sport, meat and fur. Eastern cottontails can be pests and cause damage to gardens and agricultural crops. Annual mortality is high, with an adult survival rate of about 20%. But they are prolific and considered a species of least concern. Lifespan in the wild is 1 1/2 to 2 years.

SPOONBILL

Spoonbill (Roseate Spoonbill) *Platalea ajaja*

The roseate spoonbill is one of six species of spoonbills and is the only species that lives in the western hemisphere. It lives in southern Georgia, Florida, coastal Texas and southwestern Louisiana. It is also found in coastal areas of the Caribbean, Central America, and Mexico and down to South America. In the 18th and 19th centuries, spoonbills were valued and over-hunted for their vibrant rose plumage and almost became extinct in the United States. Federal protection for spoonbills and other migratory birds in the United States was put in place with the Migratory Bird Treaty Act of 1918. Spoonbills began to recolonize Florida and Texas, and the population has now recovered.

The spoonbill is a large pink wading bird about 2 1/2 ft. tall with bright pink shoulders and rump, a white upper neck and back, long red legs and red eyes that are positioned for binocular vision. It has a spoon-shaped, spatulate bill and nostrils on the base of its bill so that it can breathe when the bill is partially submerged under water during feeding. Its head is yellowish green and partially bald as it starts losing head feathers as it ages. Juveniles are duller in color and have a full head of feathers until age three. It is thought that the spoonbill gets its distinctive pink color from the carotenoids in the crustaceans it eats.

Roseate spoonbills are social, and they roost, nest and forage in small to large colonies (up to 400) that include other wading birds such as ibises, herons and egrets. They wade and forage in shallow water (fresh, brackish or marine) in mangroves, forested swamps, mudflats and bays. While most spoonbills in the United States nest in trees and bushes, in Louisiana, some make their nests on the ground on offshore islands with colonies of birds. Spoonbills fly with deep, slow wing beats back and forth from their nests to feeding areas, and they fly in formation with legs, neck and head stretched out. Interestingly, if spoonbills on the ground see a flock of their species flying overhead, they stick their necks and bills straight up to watch, a practice called sky-gazing.

Spoonbills sleep while standing up, usually on one leg with their head tucked under a wing. They are year-round residents or short-distance migrants, depending on available food supply and water level changes.

The spoonbill is omnivorous and feeds in the early morning and evening, foraging for minnows, small crustaceans, frogs, bits of plants and insects. It does most of its feeding in shallow water, usually about 5 in. deep. It wades slowly in the water, swinging its submerged and partially open bill back and forth, often making a low guttural sound. It feels for prey, and once it finds something, it snaps its bill shut, often swallowing it whole. Spoonbills can be followed by egrets, who take advantage of the disturbed mud to find their food.

The breeding season is winter in Florida, and spring in Texas, and roseate spoonbills reach sexual maturity at 3-4 years. Courtship may involve the male bobbing its head, the pair raising wings up high, biting or crossing their bills and exchanging nest material. Pairs usually stay together for one breeding season. They pick a nesting site in the shadier sides of mangroves, trees and shrubs 5-15 ft. above water or ground. Using sticks collected by the male, the female builds a sturdy, deep nest and lines it with moss, bark and other plant materials. The clutch size is 1-5 eggs, and both parents share in the incubation (22-24 days). Newly hatched chicks have closed eyes, pink skin, sparse white down feathers, and are unable to stand. The parents feed the chicks by dribbling regurgitated food into their outstretched bills. After one month, the chicks begin moving to branches near the nest, and at six weeks, their wings are big enough to fly. The newborn chick's bill does not have the characteristic spoonbill shape, but at nine days, the bill begins to flatten, and at 39 days, it is fully shaped.

The roseate spoonbill's predators (for eggs or flesh) include alligators, coyotes, foxes, raccoons and hawks, but their biggest threat today is habitat loss. While their nesting habitats are often in protected areas like wildlife refuges, they are especially vulnerable to degradation of their foraging sites and can be disturbed by boats. Their IUCN rating is of least concern, and their lifespan in the wild is about ten years.

TURTLE

Turtle (Eastern Box Turtle) — *Terrapene carolina*

One of six *T. carolina* subspecies in North America, the eastern box turtle (*T. carolina carolina*) is a reptile found throughout the eastern half of the United States and is one of the most commonly seen turtles in the wild. Its habitat includes deciduous or mixed woodlands, fields, and neighborhoods in developed areas. It needs a water source like wetlands, a shallow pond or a stream. Its home range remains close to where it was born and is about the size of a football field. Eastern box turtles have good homing instincts and remain in their home range for their entire life. They generally are not territorial and allow other box turtles in their home range. If they are moved away from their home range, they become stressed and will continuously try to find their way back.

The eastern box turtle is about 4-8 in. long and weighs 1-2 lbs. It has a sharp, hooked beak, sturdy legs, and feet with slightly webbed clawed toes. Males usually have red eyes, and females have brown eyes. The box turtle's hearing is limited, and its ears are not external but located far behind the eyes and covered with a tympanic membrane. Its dome-like shell is dark brown or black with distinctive orange and yellow markings. The shell has three parts: a top (carapace), a bottom (plastron) and bony side bridges that join the two. Some of the eastern box turtle's skeletal parts (vertebrae, ribs, clavicles, sternum) have evolved into bony plates covered with vascular tissue that make up the underlying structure of the carapace and plastron. The bony plates are covered by keratinous outer plates (scutes) that protect and give the shell rigidity as well as its color and patterns. The box turtle's shell has nerve endings and can feel pain and bleed. If the carapace or plastron gets damaged, it can regenerate if not too severe. The plastron has a hinge located just behind the front legs that allows the turtle to shut itself completely inside when threatened (hence the name box turtle). While the turtle's colorful shell offers good camouflage, the ability to retreat into its shell is its best defense.

Shy and solitary, the eastern box turtle tends to avoid humans and other animals. It cannot adjust its body temperature internally. When cool, it can bask in the sun, or when hot, it can rest in the shade or burrow into the mud. In warmer climates, the box turtle stays active all year. During the winter in cooler climates, it finds a safe space in the hollow of a tree, in an abandoned burrow, or digs its own burrow with its hind legs where it can rest, sluggish and inactive for 3-5 months. This dormancy is similar to but different from hibernation and is called brumation for reptiles.

The eastern box turtle is an opportunistic omnivore and has an excellent sense of smell that helps it forage for insects, fruits, roots, grass, seeds, earthworms, caterpillars and flowers. Young turtles eat more animal material. When the weather is hot, box turtles eat in the early mornings to avoid the heat and dip into shallow water to cool off and find food.

Breeding season is usually spring through fall, and eastern box turtles slowly reach sexual maturity, probably about 7-10 years. Males fight for mating rights, and the strongest male wins and will often mate with several females during the season. While the female's plastron is flat, the male's is concave, which assists in mating. The male may bump the female and bite her carapace before mounting her. Mating pairs do not bond. Female turtles can store sperm for up to four years, so the female can produce a clutch of eggs without the need for a mate each year. When ready, she digs a nest hole several inches deep with her hind legs and lays 4-6 eggs and covers them. Incubation is 70-90 days, and the soil temperature determines the turtle's sex. With an ambient temperature of 72-93°F, the lower range will produce males, the higher range will produce females, and the middle range is 50/50. Once hatched, the baby turtles dig themselves out and forage for food with no help from their parents, and they are very vulnerable. The plastron hinge that closes the shell is not fully functional until age five, and with their small size and soft shell, they are easy prey.

Predators include dogs, raccoons, birds, fire ants and snakes. If a turtle gets turned onto its back, it may die if it cannot right itself. Eastern box turtles are also vulnerable to habitat loss through heavy development and construction of roads.

Many turtles are, in fact, killed in road accidents. If a turtle is observed about to cross a road, it is advised, if safe, to carry it across and set it down on the other side, facing the same direction. The eastern box turtle's IUCN rating is vulnerable, and those that reach adulthood have a lifespan of about 50 years, but some can live up to 100 years.

UNAU SLOTH

Unau Sloth (Linnaeus's Two-Toed Sloth) *Choloepus didactylus*

The unau sloth, also called Linnaeus's two-toed sloth, is found in the tropical rainforests of Central America and South America. It is arboreal and lives a solitary life in the high canopy of the rain forests with a home range of about 10 acres. Several unaus can live in similar home ranges without competing for space and food. Unaus often fall (as much as once a week) from their high homes, but they are built to withstand such falls, even up to 100', without breaking bones.

The unau is 21-29 in. long, weighs 9-17 lbs., and has long limbs and no visible tail. The front limbs have two claws (hence its name), and the back limbs have three claws. Because of its upside-down life, it is the only mammal whose hair parts from the belly and falls toward the back. Unaus have an excellent sense of smell, but their vision is weak. They see poorly in dim light and are blinded in bright light. They are good swimmers. From infancy, the unau is very strong and can lift its weight with one arm. It has a bone and muscle structure that enables its tendons to lock into place when hanging upside down from a branch. This adaptation is energy-saving and so efficient that even a dead unau can continue to hang.

The unau is probably the slowest mammal in the world. Because its diet has little nutrition, it has a low metabolism and sleeps a lot. It spends most of its time hanging motionless high up in a tree or curled up into a ball near the fork of a tree and sleeping. It can sleep 15-18 hours a day. The unau cannot control its temperature internally, so it adjusts by moving in and out of sun or shade. Its body temperature is the most variable of mammals at 74-92°F and falls when the unau is inactive or cold. If the unau gets too cold for too long, the bacteria in its stomach can stop working, and it can actually starve to death. There is a phenomenon called cold-weather orphan syndrome, where the mother unau can die of starvation while the baby continues to nurse.

Nocturnal, the unau feeds at night, eating leaves, fruit and insects, and it gets moisture from the leaves it eats. It has no incisors and uses its hardened lips to bite off leaves. Its digestive tract is very slow, and food takes a month to pass through. Unaus only need to climb down to the ground once a week to relieve themselves near the tree's base. Because they walk awkwardly and slowly, they are vulnerable to predation when on the ground. They can avoid the ground by using canopy vines to move from tree to tree, or in flooded times, they can swim to another tree.

The unau has long, grayish coarse hair, greenish in color due to algae and fungi. There is a curious ecosystem in the unau's hair that houses hundreds of moths and beetles, as well as algae and fungi. (Sloth moths are found nowhere else on earth.) When the moths die, they decompose and provide fertilizer for algae, which in turn provide the camouflage color for the sloth. When the unau makes its climb down the tree to defecate, the moths lay eggs in the dung. New moths will fly up to the canopy to colonize another unau, which completes the circle. It is thought that fungi in the unau's hair may be active against strains of bacteria, cancer and parasites, and more research is needed.

Breeding season is year-round. Males reach sexual maturity at 4-5 years, and females at 3 years. The unau is polygynous, and the male can mate with many females. When a female is ready to mate, she advertises her availability with night-time calls. If two males appear, they will fight each other while hanging on their hind legs until one wins (and the other falls). Gestation takes about six months. The mother gives birth while hanging upside down, and the precocial baby crawls onto the mother's stomach to nurse. The baby is about 10" long and weighs about 12 oz. It is weaned at five weeks and begins to hang upside down on its own at 20-25 days. The baby becomes independent of the mother at one year but may remain with the mother for two years and learn survival skills. The mother leaves part or all of her territory to the baby and moves on to get established elsewhere.

Unaus are threatened by land development and urbanization, and they are vulnerable to dog attacks and road collisions. Predators include eagles, jaguars and ocelots. They are considered a species of least concern. While it is not clear how long unaus live in the wild, it is probably 40-50 years.

VULTURE

Vulture (Black Vulture, American Black Vulture)   *Coragyps atratus*

Like their relative, the turkey vulture (distinguished by its red head), black vultures are very abundant in the Americas. They range from southeastern Canada through the eastern United States and down to Central and South America. They prefer lowlands to mountains and forage on open land. They roost in dense or scattered woods with tall trees and near a water source. They also roost on houses, buildings, and transmission towers, often waiting in the morning for the sun to heat up the air and develop thermals to assist their flying. Most black vultures are year-round residents, but some in the north may migrate south during the winter or move briefly during bad weather. They fly in flocks of several to several dozen. They often soar, and their flight pattern consists of strong, snappy wing beats followed by glides. They have adapted well to living near human habitation.

With a featherless grayish head, hooked beak and compact body, the black vulture is 22-29 in. long and weighs 3-6 lbs. It has black feathers with white under the wing tips and a wingspan of about 5 ft. It has excellent vision but a poor sense of smell. It has no vocal cords but can hiss or grunt, and it fights by pecking, biting and wing pummeling. When roosting, it often spreads its wings to catch the sun. Outside of the breeding season, black vultures are gregarious and congregate at night by the hundreds in communal roosts, often with turkey vultures. However, they are aggressive and territorial regarding food and usually do not share food except with their extended family.

Black vultures have strong family bonds and forage together for food late in the day. They almost exclusively eat carrion and often rely on turkey vultures to find it for them because of their better sense of smell. The black vultures will soar high in the sky, watching for the more solitary turkey vulture on the hunt at lower elevations. When they see it finding carrion, they will swoop down in a group to overpower and scare it off. Black vultures have weak feet and usually do not carry their food but eat on site, and a group of vultures feeding on carrion is called a wake. The vulture's head is bald and adapted to keep relatively clean when it feeds on carrion. If a water source is nearby, it may bathe after feeding.

Opportunistic omnivores, black vultures also eat fruit and vegetables and will prey on small live animals like ducks, newborn calves, and turtle hatchlings. They can hang out at urban garbage dumps and slaughterhouses as well as check highways for roadkill. Despite eating carrion, they stay healthy because they have powerful gastric acids that kill harmful bacteria, and they have a strong immune system.

Monogamous, black vultures reach sexual maturity at 3-5 years and mate for life. Breeding season is January-March in the United States. For courtship, a male may fly around a female and dive towards her. A pair may perform a display in which they perch together on a branch with wings spread and alternately jump up and down while making yapping sounds. Vultures do not build nests but choose sites in dark cavities such as hollow tree stumps, floors of caves and abandoned buildings, or on the ground under dense vegetation. A pair often returns to the same nesting site for many years, or they may perch near a potential new nesting site for several weeks, checking out its safety. The female can lay one clutch of two eggs per year, and the parents take turns incubating the eggs (32-45 days). Born helpless with downy feathers and open eyes, the hatchlings are brooded for 14 days and fed regurgitated food by the parents. In the next 24 days, they begin to eat solid food, and after 70-90 days, they are able to leave the nest. But parents often feed their young for months after fledging, and families may stay together until the next breeding season when the young are then chased from the nest. Family bonds are maintained for life. The young vultures will spend time wandering between roosts, following fellow vultures to food sites, and learning how to forage for themselves.

Black vultures are good for the environment because they clean up carrion and help prevent the spread of diseases. But they are a nuisance to farmers because they kill newborn calves. They can also damage houses and buildings, overpopulate urban garbage dumps, and threaten human safety if they fly near aircraft routes. Adult black vultures have no natural predators but are vulnerable to car collisions, and their eggs and hatchlings can be eaten by foxes, raccoons and coatis. They are federally protected by the Migratory Bird Act. The population of black vultures is stable, with an IUCN rating of least concern, and their lifespan is up to 25 years in the wild.

WOLVERINE

Wolverine (Skunk Bear) *Gulo gulo*

The wolverine lives in the polar latitudes of North America and Eurasia. The North American wolverine discussed here lives in Alaska and Canada but is also seen sporadically in the U.S. Rocky Mountains and Sierra Nevadas. Its habitat includes remote alpine forests, boreal forests, rocky areas, and arctic and subarctic tundra. Except for breeding, wolverines are solitary and do not tolerate members of the same sex. The male requires a vast territory of 200-400 square miles, and the female about 135 square miles. Male territories encompass or overlap several female territories. Wolverines give off a strong musk scent from an anal gland to mark their territory and food cache.

Furry, stocky and muscular with short legs, wolverines look like small bears with long, bushy tails. They are 14-18 in. high at the shoulder and 26-44 in. long with a 7-10 in. tail. Males weigh 24-40 lbs. and females are smaller. Wolverines have brown or black oily fur that is hydrophobic with streaks of lighter fur along the flanks. With big toes and curved retractable claws, they can walk on snow and climb trees or cliffs, and they are also good swimmers. They have a great sense of smell and good hearing but poor vision. The wolverine makes a few vocalizations, such as grunts and growls. It is shy but aggressively guards its territory and can attack fiercely if threatened.

Wolverines have tremendous physical endurance in frigid, sub-zero conditions and can travel about 15 miles a day in search of food. They are nocturnal but can also be active during the day. They make dens in caves, abandoned burrows or rock crevices and gather leaves and grass for a nest. With their thick fur, they do not need to hibernate but can make snow tunnels for protection from the cold and predators. Wolverines are intelligent and clever. They may walk on roads when available to ease their travel, and they are able to sneak bait off of scientific traps used for collaring.

Opportunistic scavengers, wolverines eat whatever is available and cache food in their den. In the winter, they can bite through bone and frozen flesh and eat carrion left by larger predators. Sometimes, they may even chase a predator away and claim the carrion. They can also catch larger prey like caribou or moose, but usually only if the animal is already weakened. They also hunt for small or medium-sized prey, and in warmer months, they will eat roots, berries, plants, seeds and eggs. With short legs, they usually do not chase prey but utilize a hide-and-pounce strategy.

Wolverines reach sexual maturity at 2-3 years. The breeding season is May-August when females are in heat. The male mates with females in his territory, and the female may also mate with males from different territories. The female, who breeds every other year, initiates the mating, and after a few days together, the pair go their separate ways. Females are induced ovulators and can delay implantation of the fertilized eggs for 2-6 months, waiting for a better time like fall or early winter or even forgoing implantation if food resources are low. After implantation, gestation is 30-50 days, and litter size is 2-3. The female digs a snow cave or den where she will give birth and stay until her kits are weaned. The den is dug very deep to protect from cold and predators and usually includes one or two long tunnels. The newborn kits are helpless, weigh less than a pound and are dependent on the mother. Weaned at three months, they can forage for themselves at 5-7 months. The father does almost no parenting but may visit with the kits periodically before they are weaned. At about one year, a male offspring will leave to begin the search to find and secure its own range. A female may stay in the mother's range for up to three years.

Large predators like bears and mountain lions are reluctant to attack the wolverine because of its ferocity, but they may attack its young. A pack of wolves is probably the most serious threat. While the wolverine population experienced a worrisome decline in the 19th century due to fur trapping, today, the numbers are fairly stable. Hunters in Alaska now harvest about 550 wolverines each year, with hunting being closely monitored and controlled by seasons and bag limits. Wolverines are currently plentiful in Alaska and Canada but are still vulnerable to climate change and habitat loss. Their population in the lower United States is very low, and hopefully, ongoing conservation efforts will help recovery. In their role of eating carrion, they are beneficial to the ecosystem. The wolverine's IUCN rating is of least concern, and its lifespan is 5-7 years in the wild and sometimes longer.

XERUS SQUIRREL

Xerus Squirrel (Unstriped Ground Squirrel) *Xerus rutilus*

The Xerus squirrel, or unstriped ground squirrel, is endemic to East Africa and is located as far north as Sudan and as far south as Tanzania. It is the only species in the Xerus genus without longitudinal stripes. It is found in dry savannas and tropical or subtropical shrublands, disturbed habitats and cultivated agricultural fields. The unstriped ground squirrel overlaps many areas with its relative, the striped ground squirrel (*X. erythropus*).

Living in loose colonies, the unstriped ground squirrel is mainly solitary and lives in a burrow alone or with one or a few others. The female's home range is 2.5-10 acres, and the male's is about 17 acres. Home ranges overlap broadly and contain multiple isolated burrow systems, which have 2-6 entrances that can be located in the shade of hanging vegetation. Unstriped ground squirrels are not territorial and are tolerant if a nonresident squirrel enters a burrow.

The unstriped ground squirrel is fossorial and well-adapted for digging burrows. It has short, coarse hair with brownish tones and a lighter front. It has a brown nose, a white patch in front of small ears and big eyes with white eye rings. Almost 9 in. tall with a 7 in. tail, it weighs 9-15 oz. Its tail is flat in appearance, and its hind legs have long white feet. Males and females look alike.

Unstriped ground squirrels spend most of their waking hours outside of their burrows. Once emerged from the burrow in the morning, they often sunbathe and groom for a while before foraging for food in open areas during the day. When hot, they take breaks and find shade to rest and cool off. They use the burrow for sleeping and shelter from predators, rain, and heat. When sensing danger, the unstriped ground squirrel can go into alert mode and stand on its hind feet to get a better look around. It can move fast and dash for the closest cover, usually a burrow or under a bush.

While not territorial, the unstriped ground squirrel has a dominance hierarchy, with males dominating over females and juveniles for food resources. They also share a pecking order with all the members of their home range. Vocalizations like chirring or chattering can occur during sexual, dominant or submissive behavior. An aggressive unstriped ground squirrel may also exhibit tail displays, posturing, and lunging. Chasing one another may also occur, but generally none of these behaviors lead to actual combat.

The unstriped ground squirrel is omnivorous and uniquely efficient in foraging, even in times when food is scarce. It may do some scatter-hoarding to cache food around its home range but mostly relies on daily foraging. It eats plants, tree fruits, seeds, eggs and insects and appears unaffected by eating poisonous tannins. It can be an agricultural pest, however, because it also eats crops like maize, ground nuts, yams and cassava. After foraging, it retreats to its burrow in the late afternoon.

Males reach sexual maturity at eight months and females at ten months. Breeding is often in March-April after the onset of the rainy season but can occur any time of the year. The male initiates mating by approaching the female with a piloerect tail arched over its back. The female reacts submissively and retreats with her tail moving up and down in quick movements. The male follows her, and eventually, the female lies prostrate on the ground for the male to mount. Before giving birth, the female establishes a natal burrow, often using an abandoned burrow, on the periphery of her home range and remains there until the pups are born and weaned. Gestation is 34 days, and the average litter size is two. The pups are born hairless with eyes closed and are cared for by the mother and weaned at ten weeks. When the mother returns to her original burrow, the pups may remain in the natal burrow until they have grown older and dispersed.

Predators include tawny eagles, jackals, snakes and lizards. Industrialization can cause habitat loss, and the unstriped ground squirrel is vulnerable to cold weather. It is not known what its lifespan is in the wild, but it can live up to six years in captivity. Its IUCN rating is of least concern, and the population remains stable.

YELLOW TANG

Yellow Tang   *Zebrasoma flavescens*

The yellow tang is a small reef-dwelling fish that lives in shallow coral reef waters (about 6-7 ft. deep) in the Pacific Ocean near the islands of Hawaii and ranging west to the Mariana Islands and Japan. It is a colorful, bright yellow fish with an ovoid shape up to 8 in. long and a narrow body less than 1 in. thick. It has a small mouth and big eyes high on its head. It has a dorsal fin with 4-5 spines and an anal fin with 3 spines. It is a member of the surgeon-fish family and has two scalpel-like spines, one on either side of its tail, that extend when the tail is flexed for defense or to fend off competitors for food and shelter. Males and females look alike, but males are usually larger.

An algae feeder, the yellow tang plays a vital role in the coral ecosystem by keeping the faster-growing algae from choking the slower-growing corals. It also provides a cleaning service to marine turtles by eating algae off of them. Diurnal, yellow tangs are often found in groups in shallow reef waters, but some may be in depths of 100 ft. or more. At night, the groups separate, and individuals take shelter in the reef crevices, their bright yellow color fading to a darker grayish yellow.

Yellow tangs become sexually active at four to seven years of age. Breeding occurs year-round, usually at the full moon, and the female can spawn about a million eggs per year. During spawning, the male changes color and exhibits a shimmering behavior. The male and female spawn in pairs or groups, and fertilization is external. No parental role is further involved, and the fertilized eggs float off to sea as plankton, unprotected and moving with the ocean currents. Next, the hatched clear planktonic larvae tang feed on the remains of the yolk and on smaller plankton. In about two months, once they have completed developing a tiny oval body with dorsal and ventral fins and spine, they are carried back by ocean currents to reefs, where they find refuge in the reef crevices and continue to grow. It is estimated that less than 1% of fertilized eggs survive this process. Juveniles tend to feed in large coral gardens where there are plenty of hiding places, and adults tend to feed in shallow reef flats where algae is very abundant. Juveniles and adults are not migratory and usually stay in the same location for many years with a home range of about 1/2 mile in diameter.

As a prize salt-water aquarium fish, the yellow tang was good for the Hawaiian economy, but problems eventually developed because of insufficient regulation, high mortality rates during collection and transportation to distant aquariums, poaching and the black market.

The yellow tang fish stock became in danger of collapsing in the 1990s. Prompted by conservationists and community concern, Hawaii began a program in 2000 to manage the species and designated nine marine protected areas (about 35% of the west coast of Hawaii) that banned commercial aquarium fishing. Since then, there has been an impressive increase in the yellow tang population in these protected areas, and studies have also indicated that some of the larval yellow tangs in open waters get dispersed as far as 100 miles away from where they had been spawned. This shows that marine protected areas do help maintain and strengthen the overall yellow tang population.

However, the issue of whether to ban or allow commercial aquarium fishing remains an ongoing and bitter debate in Hawaii. Commercial aquarium fishing is still banned, and for a while, prices for yellow tang skyrocketed. In 2015, however, after many years of effort, researchers at the Oceanic Institute in Hawaii found a way to successfully develop a captive-bred yellow tang. Today, captive-bred yellow tangs are commercially available for aquariums and at a cheaper price. This is a win-win solution for both conservation and the aquarium fish industry, and wild yellow tang can remain undisturbed in their habitat.

The yellow tang is vulnerable to habitat destruction due to coral harvesting, pollution of water, harmful fishing practices and poaching. Natural predators include larger fish, sharks, crabs, and octopuses. Its IUCN rating is of least concern, and it has a long lifespan of up to 30 years in the wild.

ZEBRA FINCH

Zebra Finch (Australian Finch, Grass Finch)   *Taeniopygia castanotis*

Once considered a single species, the zebra finch was divided into two species in 2016, the Sunda zebra finch on the Lesser Sunda Islands of Indonesia and the Australian zebra finch, discussed here. The Australian zebra finch lives in arid regions throughout most of Australia, and its habitats include scrub forests and grasslands with scattered trees and bushes, especially near water sources. They have been introduced to the U.S., Brazil, Portugal and Puerto Rico and are popular caged pets in many countries.

The zebra finch is very small at about 4 in. long and 0.5-1 oz. Both sexes have a grayish body with gray neck, white chest and abdomen, a black tail with white vertical markings, black tear-drop lines from red eyes, a reddish-orange beak, and paler orange legs and feet. In addition, the more colorful male has chestnut cheek patches, chestnut flanks with white dots, and a gray-and-black finely striped bib edged with a distinctive black chest bar. Juveniles look similar to the females but with grayish eyes and a black bill. They grow into their adult plumage 30-45 days after hatching.

Diurnal and sedentary, zebra finches are gregarious and live in large flocks of up to 100 or more. They are social and have many vocalizations, such as a loud nasal tiah (often when flying), tet, meep, beep, aha and oi. Only males sing, and members of the flock recognize each other by song. Each zebra finch's song is unique to his past. He sings original song patterns learned in early development, imitating the sounds made mostly by his father. Once an adult, the song patterns crystallize, and he can learn no new songs. He sings the original song his entire life, and the song passes from generation to generation. The female does not sing but may be attracted to a male whose song is similar to what she heard in adolescence.

Zebra finches are omnivores and fly long distances in large flocks to find food. They forage on the ground, and their diet is predominantly fallen and ripened grass seed. They can also eat fruit, vegetables and insects.

The female needs to eat insects to ensure healthy babies, and the babies need to eat insects as they grow. Accustomed to arid climates, they can go without water for long periods.

Zebra finches mature exceptionally quickly and reach sexual maturity 70-80 days after hatching. They are monogamous and pair for life, but extra-pair mating can also occur for both sexes. The breeding season can be any time and occurs after substantial rainfall. The male sings and does courtship dances to attract a mate. The pair mark their bond by perching and clumping together like a ball of feathers and preening each other. During the breeding period, the flock divides into smaller groups of about 50, but when separated, they still recognize each other by song and keep up with each other. A nesting pair is very territorial about their nest site and will only allow members of their flock to approach. Nonmembers will be chased away. The female chooses the nest site, which can be anywhere, such as in trees or bushes. The male collects nesting materials, and the pair build a loose domed nest together. The clutch can be 4-6 eggs, and both parents incubate and feed their chicks. Incubation takes two weeks, and the chicks fledge three weeks after hatching.

Predators include falcons, snakes and mice, and many small mammals will eat the eggs. The zebra finch has adapted well to human disturbances and also lives in urban areas. Because of its fast and reliable breeding and unique vocal talents, the zebra finch has become an important model species for research on vocal learning, mate choice and pair bonds. Its IUCN rating is of least concern, and its lifespan is 2-3 years in the wild and 5-7 years in captivity.

SOURCES

Alpaca

alpacabydesignshop.com/blog/what-is-the-history- of-alpacas/
"What is The History of Alpacas?" May 2023
Alpaca by Design, alpacabydesign@gmail.com
Sisters OR 97759

incaalpaca.co.uk/alpaca-info/about-alpacas/history/
"Alpaca: History"
Inca Alpaca, mail@incaalpaca.co.uk
Dorchester, Dorset,
England DT2OHU

livescience.com/52668-alpacas.html
"Facts about Alpacas" by Alina Bradford, 2017
Life Science
New York NY 10036

nationalzoo.si.edu/animals/alpaca
"Alpaca"
Smithsonian National Zoo and Conservation Biology Institute
Washington DC 20008

wikipedia.org/wiki/alpaca
"Alpaca"
Wikimedia Foundation
San Francisco CA 94104

zooatlanta.org/animal/huacaya-alpaca/"Huyacaya Alpaca"
Zoo Atlanta
Atlanta, GA 30315

Bear

adfg.alaska.gov/index.cfm?adfg=brownbear.main
"Brown Bear: Species Profile" Alaska Department of Fish and Game Juneau AK 99811

animaldiversity.org/accounts/ursus_arctos/
"Ursos arctos, brown bear" by Tanya Dewey and Liz Ballenger
University of Michigan Museum of Zoology Ann Arbor MI 48108

denaliwildlifetour.com/alaskan-wildlife/ alaskan- brown-bear/
"Alaskan Brown Bear" 2014 Doyon Tourism, Inc.
Fairbanks AK 99709

doi.gov/blog/everything-you-want-know-about- katmai-national-parks-fat-bears
"Everything You Want to Know about Katmai National Park's Fat Bears" 2023
U.S. Department of Interior
Washington DC 20240

ielc.libguides.com/sdzg/factsheets/brown- bear/ taxonomy
"Brown Bear (Ursus arctos) Fact Sheet" 2023
International Environment Library Consortium
San Diego Zoo Wildlife Alliance Library
Escondido CA 92027

nwf.org/Educational-Resources/Wildlife- Guide/Mammals/Grizzly-Bear
"Grizzly Bear"
National Wildlife Federation
Reston VA 20190

wikipedia.org/wiki/brown_bear
"Brown Bear"
Wikimedia Foundation
San Francisco, CA 94104

Cow

cattle.com/articles/title/charolais+cattle.aspx
"Charolais Cattle"
cattle.com, Spring Branch TX 78070

charolais.com/association/history/
"History" Canadian Charolais Association
Calgary AB T23 6W8

livestockpedia.com/cattle/charolais/
"Charolais"
[no other contact information]

lonepinecharolais.com/ history-and-characteristics- of-charolais-cattles/
"The History and Characteristics of Charolais Cattle" 2022
Lone Pine Charolais
Lyons, Georgia 30436

petkeen.com/charolais-cattle-breed/
"Charolais Cattle Breed," by Oliver Jones, 2023 PetKeen
Los Angeles CA 90015

Duck

allaboutbirds.org/guide/mallard/overview
"Mallard"
Cornell Lab., Cornell University
Ithaca NY 14850

a-z-animals.com/animals/mallard/
"Mallard" 2022
Flywheel Publishing, attn: A-Z Animals
Lakewood CO 80228

massaudubon.org/nature-wildlife/ birds/mallards
"Mallards"
Massachusetts Audubon Headquarters
Lincoln MA 01773

scottishwildlifetrust.org.uk/2020/03/ the-secret-life- of-mallard-ducks/
"The Secret Life of Mallard Ducks" by Amy, Visitor Centre Assistant
Scottish Wildlife Trust
Edinburgh, Scotland

wikipedia.org/wiki/mallard
"Mallard"
Wikimedia Foundation
San Francisco, CA 94104

Elephant

animaldiversity.org/accounts/loxodonta_africana/
"Loxodonta africana, African bush elephant" by Meghan Howard

University of Michigan Museum of Zoology
Ann Arbor MI 48108

elephantaidinternational.org/elephant-facts/
"Elephant Facts"
Elephant Aid International
Attapulgus GA 39815

elephantsforafrica.org/elephant-facts/
"Elephant Facts"
[no other contact information]

globalelephants.org/the-basics/
Global Sanctuary for Elephants
Brentwood, TN 37024

ielc.libguides.com/sdzg/factsheets/ african_elephant
"African Elephants"
International Environment Library Consortium
San Diego Zoo Wildlife Alliance Library
Escondido CA 92027

sheldrickwildlifetrust.org/about/ species-we-protect- elephants
"African Elephants"
Sheldrick Wildlife Trust Organization
Nairobi, Kenya

wikipedia.org/wiki/african_elephant
"African elephant"
Wikimedia Foundation
San Francisco, CA 94104

Fox

adfg.alaska.gov/index.cfm?adfg=arcticfox.main
"Arctic Fox (Alopex lagopus)"
Alaska Department. of Fish and Game
Juneaux AK 99811

animaldiversity.org/accounts/Vulpes_lagopus/
"Vulpes lagopus, Arctic fox" by Tanya Dewey and Candice Middlebrook
University of Michigan Museum of Zoology Ann Arbor MI 48108

coolantarctica.com/Antarctica%20fact%20file/ wildlife/Arctic_animals/arctic_fox.php
"Arctic Fox – Facts and Adaptations"
[no other contact information]

gov.nu.ca/sites/default/files/Arctic%20Fox.pdf
"Arctic Fox" The Government of Nunavut Iqaluit, Nunavut X0A OH

wikipedia.org/wiki/ Arctic_fox
"Arctic fox"
Wikimedia Foundation
San Francisco, CA 94104

Groundhog

a-z-animals.com/animals/groundhog-woodchuck/
"Groundhog (Woodchuck)"
Flywheel Publishing, attn: A-Z Animals
Lakewood CO 80228

hhltmaine.org/10952/nature-notes-groundhog/
"Nature Notes: Groundhog" by Ed Robinson, 2014
Harpswell Heritage Land Trust
Harpswell ME 04079

massaudubon.org/nature-wildlife/mammals-in- massachusetts/woodchucks-groundhogs
"Woodchucks (Groundhogs)"
Massachusetts Audubon Headquarters
Lincoln MA 01773

wikipedia.org/wiki/Groundhog
"Groundhog"
Wikimedia Foundation
San Francisco, CA 94104

Hippopotamus

animals.sandiegozoo.org/animals/hippo
"Hippo"
San Diego Zoo
San Diego CA 92101

a-z-animals.com/animals/hippopotamus/
"Hippopotamus" 2022
Flywheel Publishing, attn: A-Z Animals
Lakewood CO 80228

oneearth.org/species-of-the-week-hippopotamus/
"Why the hippopotamus is called the river horse" by Geraldine Patrick Encina
One Earth Foundation
Huntington Beach, CA 92649

wikipedia.org/wiki/Hippopotamus
"Hippopotamus"
Wikimedia Foundation
San Francisco, CA 94104

Ibis

allaboutbirds.org/guide/White_Ibis/overview
"White Ibis" Cornell Lab, Cornell University
Ithaca NY 14850

animaldiversity.org/accounts/Eudocimus_albus/
"Eudocimus albus, white ibis" by Jacob Mace
University of Michigan Museum of Zoology
Ann Arbor MI

marinesanctuary.org/blog/sea-wonder-white-ibis/
"Sea Wonder: White Ibis" 2020
National Marine Sanctuary Foundation Silver Spring MD 20910

wikipedia.org/wiki/American_white_ibis
"American white ibis" Wikimedia Foundation San Francisco CA 94104

Javelina

aboutanimals.com/mammal/collared-peccary/
"Collared Peccary"
aboutanimals.com
The Netherlands

desertmuseum.org/kids/oz/long-fact- sheets/Javelina.php
"Animal Fact Sheet: Collared Peccary or Javelina"
Arizona Sonora Desert Museum
Tuscon, AZ 85743

desertusa.com/animals/collared-peccary- javelina.html
"Collared Peccary – Javelina" DesertUSA
Escondido CA 92025

npshistory.com/brochures/sagu/javelina.pdf
"Javelina"
Saguaro National Park, National Park Service
Tucson AZ 85743

tpwd.texas.gov/publications/pwdpubs/media/pwd_b k_w7000_1669.pdf
"The Javelina in Texas" by Rick Taylor and David R. Synatzske
Texas Parks & Wildlife
Austin TX 78744

wikipedia.org/wiki/Peccary
"Peccary"
Wikimedia Foundation
San Francisco, CA 94104

Koala

animaldiversity.org/accounts/ Phascolarctos_cinereus/
"Phascolarctus cinerius, koala" by Jennifer Dubuc and Dana Eckroad, 1999
University of Michigan Museum of Zoology
Ann Arbor, MI 48108

cdn.environment.sa.gov.au/environment/docs/pa- fact-koalalife.pdf
"Koala life – up close and personal"
Department. Of Environment and Natural Resources Adelaide SA 5000

environment.des.qld.gov.au/wildlife/animals/living- with/koalas
"Koalas" Department of Environment and Science
Queensland Government
Brisbane QLD 4001

savethekoala.com/about-koalas/
"About Koalas"
Australian Koala Foundation, Brisbane, Queensland 4001 Australia

wikipedia.org/wiki/Koala
"Koala"
Wikimedia Foundation
San Francisco, CA 94104

Lynx

adfg.alaska.gov/index.cfm?adfg=lynx.main
"Lynx" Alaska Department. of Fish and Game
Juneaux AK 99811

animaldiversity.org/accounts/Lynx/
"Lynx" by Karter Johansen
University of Michigan Museum of Zoology
Ann Arbor MI 48108

denali.org/denalis-natural-history/lynx/
"Lynx"
Denali Education Center Denali Park AK 99755

oneearth.org/species-of-the-week-canadian-lynx/
"Canadian lynx: clever specialized hunters of the snowy forests"
by Lindsey Jean Schueman One Earth Foundation
Huntington Beach, CA 92649

wikipedia.org/wiki/Lynx
"Lynx"
Wikimedia Foundation San Francisco CA 94104

Mule

a-z-animals.com/animals/mule/
"Mule" 2023
Flywheel Publishing, attn: A-Z Animals
Lakewood CO 80228

horsetalk.co.nz/2022/06/30/romans-mules-north- central-europe-study/
"Romans brought mules north into Central Europe, study shows" 2022
Horsetalk.co.nz
info@horsetalk.co.nz

motherearthnews.com/homesteading-and-livestock/ american-mammoth-jackstock-mule-zm-0zon19zols/
"The American Mammoth Jackstock Mule" by Jeannette Beranger
Mother Earth News
Topeka KS 66609

mulemuseum.org/history-of-the-mule.html
"History of the Mule"
by David Babb American Mule Museum,
Bishop CA 93515

wikipedia.org/wiki/Mule
"Mule" Wikimedia Foundation
San Francisco CA 94104

worldanimalfoundation.org
"Mules Animal" by Caitlin Manner 2023
World Animal Foundation

Nuthatch

abcbirds.org/bird/red-breasted-nuthatch/
"Red-breasted Nuthatch"
American Bird Conservatory, Washington DC
The Plains VA 20198

allaboutbirds.org/guide/Red-breasted_Nuthatch/
"Red-breasted Nuthatch"
Cornell Lab., Cornell University
Ithaca NY 14850

animaldiversity.org
"*Sitta canadensis*, red-breasted nuthatch" by Karl Kirschbaum and Cara Sands
University of Michigan Museum of Zoology
Ann Arbor MI 48108

birdbaron.com/red-breasted-nuthatch/
"Red-Breasted Nuthatch" by Shamim1410, 2020
BirdBaron Bird Blog

hww.ca/en/wildlife/birds/red-breasted-nuthatch.html#
"Red-breasted Nuthatch" by Robert W. Nero
Hinterland's Who's Who
Kanata, Ontario K2M 2W1

wikipedia.org/wiki/Red-breasted_nuthatch
Red-breasted nuthatch" Wikimedia Foundation
San Francisco, CA 94104

Opossum

animaldiversity.org/accounts/Didelphis_virginiana/
"*Didelphis virginiana*, Virginia opossum," by Leila

S. Martina, University of Michigan Museum of Zoology
Ann Arbor MI 48108

a-z-animals.com/animals/opossum/
"Opossum" 2023
Flywheel Publishing, attn: A-Z Animals
Lakewood CO 80228

mdc.mo.gov/discover-nature/field-guide/virginia- opossum
"Opossum"
Missouri Department of
Conservation Headquarters
Jefferson City MO 65102

popsci.com/livingartifacts/#:~:text=It%20is%20mea nt%20to%20describe,very%20 few%2C%20close%20surviving%20relatives.
"Living Fossils" by Matt Ransford,
2008 Popular Science
New York, NY 10016

wikipedia.org/wiki/Opossum
"Opossum" Wikimedia Foundation
San Francisco, CA 94104

Pika

animaldiversity.org/accounts/Ochotona_princeps/
"Ochotona princeps, American pika,"
by Alexandra Peri
University of Michigan Museum of Zoology
Ann Arbor MI 48108

a-z-animals.com
"Pika, Ochotona minor" 2023
Flywheel Publishing, attn: A-Z Animals
Lakewood CO 80228

nwf.org/Educational-Resources/Wildlife-Guide/Mammals/American-Pika
"AmericanPika"
National Wildlife Foundation
Merrifield VA 22116

onekindplanet.org/animal/american-pika/
"American Pika"

One Kind Planet
Edinburgh EH7 5DL UK

wikipedia.org/wiki/American_pika
"American pika"
Wikimedia Foundation
San Francisco, CA 94104

Quail

aboutanimals.com/bird/gambels-quail/
"Gambel's Quail"
About Animals: The Online Animal
Encyclopedia The Netherlands

allaboutbirds.org/guide/Gambels_Quail
"Gambel's Quail"   Cornell Lab, Cornell University
Ithaca NY 14850

**animaldiversity.org/accounts/
Callipepla_gambelii/**
"Callipepla gambelii, Gambel's quail"
University of Michigan Museum of Zoology
Ann Arbor MI 48108

desertusa.com/birds/gambel-quail.html
"Gambel's Quail" by David B. Williams
Desert USA.
Escondido CA 92025

wikipedia.org/wiki/Gambel%27s_quail
"Gambel's Quail"
Wikimedia Foundation
San Francisco CA 94104

**www.wildlife.state.nm.us/download/conserva-
tion/ habitat-handbook/project-guidelines/
New-Mexico-Quail-Habitat-Guidelines.pdf**
"New Mexico's Quail: Biology, Distribution, and
Management Recommendations"
by L. Kamees, T. Mitchusson and M. Gruber, 2008
New Mexico Department of Game and Fish
Santa Fe NM 87507

Rabbit

**animaldiversity.org/accounts/
Sylvilagus_floridanus/**
"Sylvilagus floridanus, eastern cottontail"
by Kimberly Mikita

University of Michigan Museum of Zoology
Ann Arbor MI 48108

a-z-animals.com/animals/eastern-cottontail/
"Eastern Cottontail" 2023
Flywheel Publishing, Attn: A-Z Animals
Lakewood CO 80228

in.gov/dnr/fish-and-wildlife/wildlife-resources/ animals/cottontail-rabbit/
"Cottontail Rabbit"
Indiana Dept. of Natural Resources
Indianapolis IN 46204

massaudubon.org/nature-wildlife/ mammals-in- massachusetts/cottontail-rabbits
"Cottontail Rabbits"
Massachusetts Audubon Headquarters Lincoln MA 01773

wikipedia.org/wiki/Eastern_cottontail
"Eastern cottontail" Wikimedia Foundation
San Francisco CA 94104

Spoonbill

allaboutbirds.org/guide/Roseate_Spoonbill/ overview
"Roseate Spoonbill" Cornell Lab,
Cornell University
Ithaca NY 14850

audubon.org/field-guide/bird/roseate-spoonbill
"Roseate Spoonbill," by Kenn Kaufman
National Audubon Society
New York NY 10014

a-z-animals.com/animals/roseate-spoonbill/
"Roseate Spoonbill" 2023
Flywheel Publishing, attn: A-Z Animals
Lakewood CO 80228

evergladesfoundation.org/post/ the-tale-of-the-rose- colored-spoonbill
"The Tale of the Rose Colored Spoonbill,"
by Dr. Ruscena Wiederholt
The Everglades Foundation
Palmetto Bay FL 33157

nationalzoo.si.edu/animals/roseate-spoonbill
"Roseate Spoonbill"
Smithsonian National Zoo and Conservation Biology Institute
Washington DC 20008

wikipedia.org/wiki/Roseate_spoonbill
"Roseate spoonbill" Wikimedia Foundation
San Francisco, CA 94104

Turtle

a-z-animals.com/animals/eastern-box-turtle/
"Eastern Box Turtle" 2023
Flywheel Publishing, attn: A-Z Animals
Lakewood CO 80228

ncwildlife.org/Portals/0/Learning/documents/ Profiles/Reptile/Box_Turtle_Wildlife_Profile_ UPDA TE_2018.pdf
"Eastern Box Turtle,"
by Kimberly Burge and Melissa Jones,
N.C.Wildlife Resources Commission
Raleigh NC 27699

nwf.org/Educational-Resources/Wildlife-Guide/Reptiles/Eastern-Box-Turtle
"Eastern Box Turtle"
National Wildlife Federation
Merrifield VA 22116

totalreptile.com/ do-turtles-have-nerves-in-their- shells/
"Do Turtles Have Nerves in Their Shells"
[no other contact information]

welcomewildlife.com/all-about-box-turtles/
"All about box turtles"
Site hosted by Soteria Technology Solutions
[no other contact information]

wikipedia.org/wiki/Eastern_box_turtle
"Eastern box turtle" Wikimedia Foundation
San Francisco, CA 94104

Unau Sloth

animalia.bio/ linnaeuss-two-toed- sloth?taxonomy=492
"Linnaeus's two-toed sloth"
info@animalia.bio

animals.sandiegozoo.org/animals/two-toed-sloth
"Two-toed Sloth"
San Diego Zoo
San Diego CA 92101

discovermagazine.com/planet-earth/the-furry-ecosystem-of-algae-moths-and-sloth-feces
"The Furry Ecosystem of Algae, Moths, and Sloth Feces"
by Darren Incorvaia, 2022 Discover Magazine Headquarters
Waukesha WI 53187

nationalzoo.si.edu/animals/two-toed-sloth
"Two-Toed Sloth"
Smithsonian National Zoo and Conservation Biology Institute,
Washington DC 20008

slothconservation.org/10-incredible-facts-about- the-sloth/
"top 10 incredible facts about the sloth" by Dr. Rebecca Cliffe

The Sloth Foundation
contact@slothconservation.org

wikipedia.org/wiki/Linnaeus%27s_two-toed_sloth
"Linnaeus's two-toed sloth"
Wikimedia Foundation
San Francisco CA 94104

Vulture

allaboutbirds.org/guide/Black_Vulture/lifehistory
"Black Vulture, Life History" Cornell Lab.,
Cornell University
Ithaca NY 14850

animaldiversity.org/accounts/Coragyps_atratus/
"Coragyps atratus, black vulture" by Glen Elliott
University of Michigan Museum of Zoology
Ann Arbor MI 48108

animalspot.net/black-vulture.html
"Black Vulture"
[no other contact information]

dnr.sc.gov/wildlife/publications/nuisance/vultures.pdf
"Vultures" South Carolina Department of Natural Resources, Columbia SC 29201

hawkmountain.org/raptors/black-vulture
"Black Vulture" and "Meet the Black Vulture"
Hawk Mountain Sanctuary
Kempton PA 19529

wikipedia.org/wiki/Black_vulture
"Black vulture"
Wikimedia Foundation
San Francisco CA 94104

Wolverine

adfg.alaska.gov/index.cfm?adfg=wolverine.main
"Wolverine *(Gulo gulo)*"
Alaska Department. of Fish and Game"
Juneaux AK 99811

animaldiversity.org/accounts/Gulo_gulo/
"*Gulo gulo*, wolverine" by Liz Ballenger, Matthew Sygo and Vincent Patsy
University of Michigan Museum of Zoology
Ann Arbor MI 48108

a-z-animals.com/animals/wolverine/
"Wolverine: Gulo gulo"2023
Flywheel Publishing, attn: A-Z Animals
Lakewood CO 80228

wikipedia.org/wiki/Wolverine
"Wolverine" Wikimedia Foundation
San Francisco, CA 94104

worldanimalfoundation.org/advocate/wild-animals/params/post/1292173/wolverines
"Discovering the Solitary World of the Wolverine Animal!" by Nicky Hoseck, 2023
World Animal Foundation
info@worldanimalfoundation.org

Xerus Squirrel

animaldiversity.org/accounts/Xerus_rutilus/
"Xerus rutilus, unstriped ground squirrel," by Isabel Martinez-Welgan
University of Michigan Museum of Zoology
Ann Arbor MI 48108

gbif.org/species/2437455
"Xerus rutilus (Cretzschmar, 1828)
Global Biodiversity Information Facility
Copenhagen Denmark

scientificlib.com/en/Biology/Animalia/ Chordata/ Mammalia/XerusRutilus01.html
"Xerus rutilus" by Martina Nicolls
Scientific Library, hellenicaworld@gmail.com

usgs.gov/publications/ home-range-social- behavior-and-dominance-relationships-african-unstriped-ground
"Home range, social behavior, and dominance relationships in the African unstriped ground squirrel, *Xerus rutilus*," by Thomas J. O'Shea, 1976 abstract U.S. Geological Survey
Reston VA 20192

wikipedia.org/wiki/Unstriped_ground_squirrel
"Unstriped ground squirrel"
Wikimedia Foundation
San Francisco, CA 94104

Yellow Tang

animaldiversity.org/accounts/ Zebrasoma_flavescens/
"Zebrasoma flavescens" by Kara Zabetakis
University of Michigan Museum of Zoology
Ann Arbor MI 48108

ncei.noaa.gov/data/oceans/coris/library/ NOAA/ CRCP/other/grants/ NA10NOS4100062/6_ FISHLIFE_YellowTang.pdf
"As Fishing Increases, Yellow Tangs Flourish. What Gives?" by Scott Radway National Centers for Environmental Information NOAA, ncei.info@noaa.gov

reefbuilders.com/2015/10/20/ yellow-tangs-finally-captive-bred-oceanic-institute/ "Yellow tangs finally captive bred by the Oceanic Institute" by Jake Adams, 2015
Reef Builders
Wilmington DE 19801

sharkstewards.org/kona-gold-the-yellow-tang/
"Kona Gold: The Yellow Tang"
Berkeley CA 94704

waikikiaquarium.org
"Yellow Tang" Waikiki Aquarium
Honolulu HI 96815

wikipedia.org/wiki/Yellow_tang
"Yellow Tang" 2023 Wikimedia Foundation
San Francisco, CA 94104

Zebra Finch

animaldiversity.org/accounts/Taeniopygia_guttata/
"Taeniopygia guttata, zebra finch"
by Rossi White University of Michigan
Museum of Zoology
Ann Arbor MI 48108

animalspot.net/zebra-finch.html
"Zebra Finch"
[no other contact information]

australian.museum/learn/animals/birds/zebra-finch-taeniopygia-guttata/
"Zebra Finch" by Melissa Murray, 2020 Sydney
NSW 2010, Australia

cs.cmu.edu/afs/cs/academic/class/15883- f13/lectures/birdsong/finches.html
"Zebra Finches"
Carnegie Mellon University School of
Computer Science
Pittsburgh PA 15213

psy.fsu.edu/~johnson/johnsonlab/johnson.htm
"The Animal We Study"
The Johnson Lab, Florida State University,
Tallahassee FL 32306

wikipedia.org/wiki/Zebra_finch
"Zebra Finch" 2023
Wikimedia Foundation
San Francisco CA 94104